BREEDING DISCUS
A YEARBOOK
TODAY

All you need to know to successfully breed Discus from the field's leading authority in Germany. Completely illustrated with informative color photographs.

BERND DEGEN

With a special chapter on artificial fry raising by Jack Wattley, America's leading Discus breeder.

PUBLISHER'S NOTE

The Germans have impressed the discus world with the quality and quantity of top notch discus they have produced. Herr Degen is Germany's outstanding breeder of fancy strains, so we translated his book because he kept no secrets. It's all here . . . everything you need to know. We have added the last chapter on "Things You Need for Successful Discus Breeding" because most German products are not available in the outside world.

The names for some of the varieties may be different from those familiar to you. Almost every geographical area has its own name for many color varieties of discus. We have used the American names used in the New York metropolitan area whenever possible.

The magnificent chapter by Jack Wattley discloses his secrets of raising Discus without their parents.

Translated by
U.Erich Friese
Aquarium & Zoo
Consultant
Sydney, Australia

Copyright 1996 For English Language edition by T.F.H. Publications, Inc.

Copyright 1995 bede-Verlag GmbH, Bühlfelderweg 12, 94239 Ruhmannsfelden

Photo source: All illustrations bede-Verlag archives, unless otherwise indicated.

CONTENTS

A. Shirase's pigeon blood discus with fry. This strain is easy to maintain and Shirase's fish are in magnificent condition, as you can see. Photo by Y. Nakamura from *Discus Yearbook, '91-'92*, in Japanese.

Fumitoshi Mori took this magnificent photo of a discus aquarium. This kind of aquarium could be in your own home! From *Discus Yearbook, '91-'92* in Japanese.

Hardly any other freshwater fish has so been taken into the hearts of aquarists as the discus. Although these kings of the Amazon were discovered more than 100 years ago, it was not until after the Second World War that they conquered Europe. The foundations for selective (pedigree) breeding of discus was laid in the United States and, more specifically, in Germany. In doing so, dedicated discus breeders have succeeded in sending the kings of the Amazon on a triumphant journey around the entire world. Through the development of highly selected strains, these fish have become world famous among aquarists. 'Discus fever' went around the world and continues unabated among discus hobbyists to this day.

Breeding these majestic fish and possibly producing new color varieties is still a challenge for aquarists. While discus breeding in the United States and in Europe was already at its peak during the 1960's, it was still in its infancy in Southeast Asian countries. The market significance of discus was slow to be recognized among Asians. But then countries like Singapore and Thailand responded very quickly to the demand for discus. Consequently, in the early 1970's many discus were already being exported to Europe and to the United States; however, the quality of these fish did not meet the expectations of spoiled German discus fanciers. While the European aquarists wanted the intensely colored turquoise varieties, the Asians could supply only brown discus. But soon, after some initial setbacks, the Southeast Asian discus breeders succeeded in acquiring highly colored breeding stock from overseas in order to produce better color varieties of discus. By means of careful, selective breeding and critical selection of the new progeny, these countries also produced, very quickly, quality turquoise discus. And so gradually a large export market for discus was established in Southeast Asian countries. Today discus of many color varieties are exported in huge numbers from there to all parts of the world.

Discus production in Asia is distinctly different from that in Europe or the United States. The climate and economic situation in Southeast Asia enable breeders there to set up large breeding facilities under very basic operating conditions. On the other hand, breeders in Europe and the United States have to confine themselves, more or less, to hobby breeding of discus, since the ideal external conditions are absent. Consequently, discus

breeders in Europe confine their activities primarily to the production of classic, well-established discus varieties, while their Southeast Asian counterparts tend to cross everything that will naturally interbreed. This then produces new color varieties, which may not always be genetically stable. Yet, it can also lead to surprising breeding results, most recently, the 'Pigeon Blood' discus, which has excited the entire discus fraternity.

Breeding discus should remain a hobby and not be degraded as a source of monetary gain. Let us enjoy

discus breeding success together, but also let us make every effort to maintain these fish in their natural beauty, and lastly let us not forget to protect their habitats in Amazonia. In fact, habitat protection is now more important than ever before. Fortunately, in the Rio Negro region, nature has not yet been unduly affected and viable discus habitats still exist there. Regrettably, though, in many other parts of Amazonia there has already been massive destruction of the natural habitats of these fish due to over-exploitation of nature.

The world-famous fish specialist Dr. Herbert R. Axelrod comes to Germany regularly, and then inevitably visits his friend Bernd Degen. Dr. Axelrod is internationally known for his discoveries of many aquarium fish species. The brown discus is named in his honor.

OUTFITTING THE DISCUS AQUARIUM

You can't decide on the size of the tank you need until you make a decision about the quantity and size of the discus you are going to put into it. A discus tank can't be too large; it can only be too small. A 55 gallon tank, with filters and aeration, should not contain more than six adult fish (like the two shown here).

TANKS AND TANK SIZES

Before selecting a tank, it is important to decide what exactly it is going to be used for. If it is only for keeping discus without breeding them, it is advisable to buy a tank with a minimum length of 48 inches. Height and width of the tank should be at least 18 inches. Such a tank, with a volume of 55 gallons, can easily be used to raise eight to ten discus. For adult discus the number should be limited to six fish. If more fish are to be kept, it is advisable to select a larger tank.

Smaller tanks are quite adequate for breeding discus. A standard size for a discus breeding tank could, for instance, be a cuboidal shape of 20 x 20 x 20 inches, but this is of course only one of many possibilities. On the other hand, there is nothing stopping us from keeping a pair in a slightly larger tank for breeding purposes. Established, well-bonded pairs with a good brood care record will raise their young even in larger tanks of, say, 40 to 48 inches in length. Yet for young, inexperienced pairs, breeding tanks with capacities of 20 to 30 gallons have proven to be ideal. In such compact tanks the young must have close contact to their parents, which ultimately has a positive effect, especially during the first few days of their life.

In essence, the classical discus tank has volume of 20 to 30 gallons and does not contain any kind of substrate. The only pieces of decor are the typical discus spawning cones or other objects for depositing eggs on. Discus breeding tanks must always be without decoration because they are far easier to clean. Cleanliness and cleaning of the breeding tank play an important part which must not be underestimated. For discus breeders with several tanks such 'sterile' set-ups provide significant time-saving.

Yet, it is also possible for a dedicated, occasional breeder

Typical discus breeding set-up commonly found in many German basements. The breeding tanks are not particularly large and have as a center piece the typical spawning vase or cone. Usually the breeding tanks are positioned at eye level, while the rearing tanks below do not need to be at the focal point of attention.

Artificial root structures, made of clay or ceramic, have proven to be useful and are available through pet stores. Under no circumstances must such roots cause the aquarium water to give off even a mild odor of decay. They must be removed immediately, if even the slightest odor is detected.

Large stones can also be used as decorative items or as spawning substrate. Since discus often prefer to spawn on sloping, long surfaces it is recommended to place rock tiles as decoration in to a discus breeding tank. It is important, however, that these rocks do not give off any hardening agents into the water because changes in water hardness can conceivably have a negative influence on the development of discus eggs. The most suitable tiles or rock slabs, for instance, are those of granite or slate.

During the breeding season discus kept in an aquarium will spawn on all sorts of objects. If there is no suitable spawning substrate, e.g. a spawning cone, the fish will, out of necessity, attach their eggs to rod heaters or simply to the glass sides of the tank. Commercial hatcheries in Asia simply place bricks as spawning substrates into discus breeding tanks. Since the reader will most likely wish to combine discus breeding with more aesthetic considerations, it is probably more advisable to select a more decorative spawning substrate.

As mentioned earlier on, discus breeding tanks generally do not contain any kind of bottom substrate so that left-over food and fecal matter can easily be siphoned out daily,

to set up his tanks a bit more attractively. Maybe you would gladly put up with the extra work involved; then there is nothing really to stop you from adding a few decorative touches to the breeding tank. One variation, for instance, would be the introduction of an Amazon swordplant into the tank, planted in a pot filled with gravel. This way there may not be any bottom

substrate in the tank, but then it contains at least an attractive decorative plant. Sometimes discus will even spawn on these plants.

There is, of course, also the possibility of introducing tree root into a discus breeding tank; however, a certain caution is advisable, because roots can give off substances which could conceivably have a negative effect on the water.

Discus feel very secure in a tank decorated with plants and roots. Their magnificent colors are particularly effective in such a display tank.

The typical breeding tanks do not contain any bottom substrate in order to facilitate cleaning. The clay vase is generally well-accepted as spawning substrate by all discus pairs. As we can see, this pair has decided to spawn on the cone. Photo: Gilbert.

not be too coarse. It is important to use only a few individual plants. If we then stick an aquarium background decal to the outside of the back glass panel we get a very attractive diorama-effect for this breeding tank. Feeding should take place principally in the front half of the tank, where there is no substrate and from where any accumulated debris can easily be siphoned out. The back part of the aquarium with plants and bottom substrate will then convey to the viewer a largely natural picture; moreover, the discus will feel comfortable in such a tank. A spawning cone should be positioned in the 'hygienic' front section of the aquarium.

Another possibility is to have a bottom substrate in a breeding tank is as follows:

The thoroughly cleaned substrate is dried out meticulously and the bottom panel is covered (painted) with a thick layer of silicone sealant. This must, of course, be a type of silicone which is suitable for aquarium purposes. Before the silicone 'sets', it is covered with a layer of dry sand, which is then pressed slightly into the silicone so that it will solidly adhere. The silicone will harden in a few hours and after that the tank can be held upside-down, so that all sand not adhering to the silicone falls out. When using brown silicone we even get an additional shading effect. The sand layer sticking to the silicone now remains in the tank and forms a natural bottom substrate. The latter becomes solidly bonded to the tank, so that food remnants can easily be siphoned off the bottom. This provides discus in a

so dirt does not accumulate in corners and along the bottom of the tank. A minimum of cleanliness is required at all times, since discus eggs can easily become infected with fungus. Still there is a possibility to make a discus breeding tank more attractive without having to sacrifice easy cleaning, by using the following 'tricks': install a glass strip down the center of the tank from left to right,

using an appropriate (inert) aquarium sealant. This 2 to 3 inch high glass strip divides the aquarium into a front and back section. The bottom of the back section is then covered with sand or gravel to a depth reaching to the edge of the glass strip. Of course, this bottom substrate must be thoroughly disinfected. Then a few decorative plants are placed into this substrate, which — incidentally — must

Discus will also spawn on plants, provided their leave are sufficiently large. This cobalt-blue discus pair feels very much at home in this well-decorated tank. Consequently, there is little to prevent them from successfully breeding here.

This photograph shows that various other items can also be used for effectively decorating discus tanks. Discus feel very secure among the roots and plants. Large roots must be closely inspected; they must not be allowed to give off excessive amounts of decaying substances into the aquarium water. Otherwise there is a rapid build up of an organic load in the water, much to the detriment of the fish. Under these conditions, discus have a tendency to turn very dark. Photo: Lauryssens.

breeding tank with a hygienic, as well as a natural-appearing, bottom.

Sometimes fighting breaks out between a male and female, which may lead to injuries. In small breeding tanks the attacked partner does not have any places to hide and has to endure physical abuse. For that reason it is important to physically separate the two partners for a short period. Usually it is the female which is pursued aggressively, especially if she is not yet ready to spawn. In such a situation it is best to transfer the female for a while to another tank. Normally, after a few days she can be returned again to the male, and usually domestic tranquillity returns; however, should this not be the case it is advisable to remove the male. After a few days he is then returned to the female. This procedure has the advan-

tage that the female will settle into the tank and then the male becomes the new arrival. Usually the male then adopts a more conciliatory attitude towards the female. Setting up specific hiding places in a breeding tank usually fails due to the small size of the tank. Establishing territories through the use of decorative objects, which then provides sanctuary to a pursued fish, can really only be done in sufficiently large tanks.

A question which keeps coming up is: can discus be bred in an established planted aquarium? This is, of course, quite possible; however, it is more difficult than in a sterile breeding tank. A well-established planted aquarium usually contains other fishes too, which can become predators of discus eggs and young. Consequently one would have to expect that some of the young discus will be eaten by

Below Left: Discus can feel uncomfortable in an undecorated tank when there are no hiding places. Even adding just a single root or a spawning pot will provide some security. This fully-grown discus takes advantage of this situation by using the root as cover against the photographer. It is especially important for pairs to have tank decor such as roots or spawning pots, in order to provide the submissive partner an opportunity to get away from the aggressor.

Below Right: If you do not wish to put sand on the bottom, but still like to see some plants in the discus tank you can use individually potted plants. This breaks up the monotonous picture and allows the fish to establish territories.

Again a typical example of the combination spawning pot and well-decorated planted aquarium. Although planting is only sparse in this tank, the fish feel immediately more comfortable and secure. For breeding, the fish will certainly accept the spawning pot as substrate for their eggs. As far as the bottom substrate in this tanks is concerned, it should be noted here that this should not be as coarse as seen in this picture. Fine sand prevents the penetration of left-over food particles and waste products, which quickly starts to decay and pollute the water. Fine sand is distinctly prevalent as bottom substrate in the rivers of Amazonia.

Why don't you try potting a well-developed Amazon swordplant into a breeding tank! The fish will be grateful to you and may even spawn on the leaves of that plant or on the flowerpot if is large enough. The discus brood would then have an opportunity later on to graze algae off the plant leaves.

the other tank inhabitants. In large planted aquariums, on the other hand, young discus will be able to find a lot of micro-organisms as food, which then simplifies their rearing. Normally what happens in a planted aquarium is that the discus pair looks for a territory to deposit their eggs, and then starts the spawning site preparation. If the discus eggs are not eaten by other fish in the tank, the larvae will indeed hatch. In a planted aquarium it is, of course, important that water conditions are suitable for breeding discus. In a planted aquarium, it often happens that all of the eggs end up covered with fungus. There can be several reasons for this. On one hand there may be unsuitable water conditions, and on the other hand there may also be high bacteria population densities present. If the pair actually manages to get it's eggs hatched and the young larvae are swimming with their parents, they will defend their young quite aggressively against the other tank occupants. Once the first (critical) period has been overcome, the young fish will — at first hesitantly — periodically move away to explore the rest of the tank. Depending upon the size and species of the other tank occupants, that is the point in time when predation on young discus may occur.

From that point on feeding the young discus must take place in a highly deliberate and specific manner, e.g. feeding newly hatched brine shrimp (*Artemia*) by 'blowing' the brine shrimp with a long hose directly among the young discus.

This discus seems to feel far more comfortable in this decorated tank than in a sterile holding tank, as is commonly done. Of course, a decorated tanks is more labor-intensive than a sterile holding tank, but maybe the effort is indeed worthwhile. Photo: Hirsch.

If, in terms of size and decoration, the tank can be divided into half by installing a plastic-coated wire screen, it is advisable to do so. To do that you build a frame for this partition and install it in such a way that the discus pair (and its young) are in one half of the tank and the other tank occupants are in the other. This way you avoid having the young discus fall prey to the other fish.

Of course, you can also let the discus brood grow up naturally. After all, in nature not all discus larvae reach maturity either. It is very interesting to rear a discus brood in a large planted aquarium and observe the natural development in such a community tank. However, if your discus breeding attempts in a community tank never get beyond the spawning stage, you might decide one day to transfer the pair to a dedicated breeding tank. Once the adults have started to spawn regularly, they will continue to do so even in another tank.

Every discus aquarium must be properly covered, because discus are capable jumpers. This is especially true with sudden changes in light levels from dark to bright, as fright reactions occur easily among discus. Please do not underestimate this sort of reaction, because many aquarists have lost fish due to jumping. In order to avoid this, it is advisable to leave a night light burning in a room where the discus are kept. The installation of low wattage lights directly above breeding tanks has also proven to be very effective. The aquarium trade now offers various models of such economy lamps, which are easy to install. Aquarists that are technically inclined can even install an automatic

Below: This photograph demonstrates that discus breeding can be successful in a decorated tank as shown in this photograph. This pair and its young inhabit a tank which is 3 feet long, 20 inches high and 20 inches wide. The pair has spawned repeatedly in this tank and has reared its young to a size of 3 cm, when they were transferred to a grow-out tank. Since there were no other fish in this aquarium, losses among the young discus were kept at a minimum.

dimmer switch, so that the tank lights are gradually lowered at night and raised again at dawn. Daylight is ideal for breeding rooms, so that artificial lighting can be controlled via daylight sensors. In such a situation artificial lighting would be inferior to daylight. At the onset of dusk the aquarium room will become gradually darker. This provides a natural dusk light level for the fish. At dawn the artificial lighting is not turned on until there is already sufficient diffuse light in the aquarium room. This way, the discus are being gradually adapted to a light / dark rhythm. But even with precise lighting control the tank surface must be covered. This does not only prevent discus from jumping, but also cuts down significantly on electricity consumption. The various cut-out sections in the

Left:
The dream of every discus fancier surely must be a large, well-planted display aquarium in the living room. If you want to set up such tank, the discus which eventually are going to live in this tank must be thoroughly checked for disease symptoms and be adequately quarantined. Treating discus in a large, decorated tank for diseases is extremely difficult and has little — if any — chance of success. Small discus are not suited for such a display tank because they need to be fed several times a day, and left-over food would quickly pollute the water. Moreover, finding and removing left-over food is very difficult. Therefore, it is advisable to use sub-adult or adult discus, but please note that discus are actually schooling fish. Do not make the mistake and place only two or three large discus in such a tank. A display tank of 50 to 70 gallons volume can easily accommodate 6 to 10 fully grown discus. You will then also find that there is hardly any aggression among discus when they are kept in a large group.

cover glass accommodating filter stems, pipes, heaters, etc. must not be too large. Frightened juvenile discus in particular can jump through the narrowest of gaps.

LIGHTING

It is not difficult to configure the correct lighting for a discus tank, because fluorescent tubes have proven to be the most effective for this purpose. Although it is often claimed that discus require only low light levels, this is not the case. In the wild, discus live in sun-flooded waters of the Amazon river

Right:
The combination of potted plants and a sterile bottom was also chosen for this tank. It immediately gives the tank a more pleasant appearance and the bottom is still easy to clean. The discus shown here have turned in to magnificent specimens. Photo: Wouters.

system. The reason why discus hobbyists are being advised to provide diffuse light for their fish, maybe that discus kept in sterile tanks (no hiding opportunities) and under bright illumination, tend to react in panic to any shadow falling over the tank. Therefore, positioning the tank correctly seems to me to be more important than diffuse lighting. Beyond that, a tank set up next to an entry door is in a less favorable position than one in a far corner of the room. Moreover, a tank should not be too close to the floor, but always at least 25 inches above it. It is also easier for an observer if the fish swim at eye level.

Fluorescent tubes provide ideal lighting for keeping discus, especially since they

Above: Normally discus are bred in undecorated ('sterile') tanks, and of course without bottom substrate. This makes water hygiene easier, possibly creating conditions under which more young discus can be raised than in a decorated tank. In this tank roots from an overhead plant are growing into the water below. Roots remove some of the nitrate in the water, but in a tank with such a large fish population this is of little significance. In this situation a daily partial water change is unavoidable, because the metabolic waste products from that many young discus place a substantial organic load on to the water. In addition, left-over food must be siphoned out every evening. This then automatically provides for a small partial water change. Photo: Hoffmann.

Facing Page: Discus tend to become frightened easily, especially when there are unfavorable lighting conditions around the tank. If some light falls on to the tank through a door left ajar or when there are too many light sources outside the tank, which can throw shadows in to the aquarium, there can be flight reactions. These are totally natural and are not automatically indicative of disease. On the other hand, healthy discus should be sufficiently conditioned to humans and recognize when food is brought to the tank. This photograph shows clearly that discus prefer to stay under a root where they feel more secure. This 'artificial' root is made of glazed earthenware. As soon as discus are given the opportunity to hide, they will do so. This must be taken into consideration when decorating a tank. If tanks are planted too heavily, the fish have a tendency to hide among the plants. Therefore, it is advisable to use only low-growing plants and only a few solitary plants at that.

are available in different light colors. Aquarists tend to prefer lights with strong red tones, as for instance in the well-known gro-lux tubes, which enhance the shades of red in discus. Of course,

ultimately it is up to the taste of the individual with what color shade he wishes to influence the coloration of his discus. Mercury vapor lights, the so-called HQI or HQL lamps are less suitable for

discus, because these high intensity lights give a some-what cold appearance to the brilliant colors of discus.

LARGE BREEDING FACILITY

Many discus hobbyists would like to set up a large breeding facility. If the re-quired space is available, it is not difficult to operate such discus breeding venture in a cost-effective way. Since the tank water must be heated to a temperature of 82 - 86° F, such a room must be well-insulated. Before setting up the support stands with their respective tanks, the room must be closely checked out for its potential. The availabil-ity of a water supply and appropriate drainage would be ideal; this makes changing water that much easier. Even better yet would be a floor drain in this room so that any spilled water can be pushed in it with a mop or floor squee-gee. It would also be highly advantageous if the room has central heating. It keeps the air drier when the radiator is on during the cold months of the year. Many professional discus breeders insist on such space heating. It also keeps humidity down, which other-wise could lead to structural damages. But it is also impor-tant that there is sufficient ventilation (fresh air). If you are considering using a room in the basement which has no direct contact to the outside via a window, you may wish to consider installing a ventila-tion duct.

There are actually small ventilators available for win-dow- and wall penetrations, which can be built directly into a window or wall. An electric timer can be used to

In this case we find HQL lamps suspended above an uncovered aquarium. Having the large display plants grow out and above the aquarium makes for a very aesthetic appearance. An inherent disadvantage is, of course, substantial evaporative loss of tank water, which must be heated to at least 82° F for keeping discus. When adding make-up water it is important that this water is as soft as possible. Hard water causes carbonate deposits along the water's edge, which are difficult to remove.

control the operating periods of such a ventilator, which then facilitates fresh air intake.

As with other electrical installations in a fish breeding room, special attention must be paid to the fact that all fittings and associated equipment are exposed to high humidity; in essence the fittings must be adequately waterproof, and there must also be appropriate circuit breakers.

Setting up a discus breeding facility in a dedicated room

Right: In order to supply the breeding facility with water of high quality, large volumes of water are preconditioned or prepared for breeding purposes in separate vats. With the aid of filters — some of them filled with peat moss or other filter media, the desired pH and water hardness is established. This water is then pumped from the vats directly into the breeding tanks.

Below: Fluorescent tubes provide the ideal illumination for a discus aquarium, but suspended HQL lamps are also popular for large display tanks which are open, permitting the plants to grow out of the tank.

assumes that the tanks are to be placed on stands on sufficiently strong shelves. Some breeders prefer to 'stack' the tanks above each other, while other strongly advise against two-tiered tank arrangements. Both systems have advantages as well as disadvantages. 'Stacking' tanks has the advantage of providing additional space to accommodate more tanks over a given floor area. But a distinct disadvantage of such an arrangement is that the working height becomes more inconvenient. Consequently, you may well need a chair or step ladder when servicing (feeding/cleaning) the upper row of tanks. Another disadvantage of this system is that the lower tanks are too close to the floor and fish may become very shy (shadow effect—see above), but other factors may also come in to play here. If there is a lot of 'traffic' in the breeding room, fish in the lower

This is a large breeding facility, which is partially serviced by a central filter. The disadvantage of central filtration is, of course, the problem of disease transmission from one tank to the others. Therefore, it is abso—lutely mandatory that newly aquired fish be given a prolonged and meticulous quarantine treatment.

(and upper) tanks will quickly adapt to the constant movement and will quickly lose their shyness. When selecting stands or install shelving one has to take in to consideration that a full tank is quite heavy. Ready-made shelving from building suppliers do not always meet these special requirements, by including an appropriate safety margin. Therefore, select only sufficiently stable shelving so that there will not be a disaster.

Steel or angle iron shelving needs to be appropriately treated and painted to avoid rust formation. Admittedly, in a damp aquarium room this difficult to avoid. One alternative here would be to use aluminium shelving which is also available, but at a higher cost.

Apart from shelving made of metal there is also wooden shelving, but this must be water-proofed with lacquer or similar substance so that the wood will not soak up moisture and then swell up. Compressed wood chip or similar panels (e.g.masonite) used in conjunction with wooden shelving are not suitable since they will sooner or later always swell up. An inexpensive alternative is to use concrete blocks as tank support; there is really no limit to what can be used, provided there is always sufficient structural strength because water is heavy.

If the required filtration is going to be located underneath the tanks, this must be taken into consideration when building the shelves, as well as the fact that filters must be accessed frequently for servicing. There is even the possibility of installing the filtration unit(s) on a mobile platform which can be pushed in and out of the space below the tanks. Again, there are no limits to the imagination.

Once the stand or shelf has been suitably prepared, the breeding tanks can be set up. Between tank bottom and shelf there must be some sort of padding which insulates and levels the tank. Ideal for that purpose are styrofoam panels about 3/5 inch thick. This saves energy and also

levels the tank (and so minimizes structural tension).

Select breeding tanks with a minimum length of 24 inches. Such a tank has a volume of 20 gallons, but this must be the lower limit. It is up to personal taste whether to vary the size of breeding tanks, but more than 55 gallons is not advisable for a breeding tank. Once the tanks have been selected a decision needs to be made whether to filter each tank individually or whether a single filter is to service all tanks used. Clearly, filtering each tank separately has the advantage that the respective tank can be serviced individually and possible disease outbreaks are not transmitted to other tanks. A disadvantage of individual filtration lies in the fact that only a relatively small volume of water forms a biological unit. For instance, it is difficult to maintain a constant pH level in these individual tanks. If several breeding tanks are interconnected by a central filtration unit, the joint water volume of these tanks then acts as a single biological entity. This then makes it essentially easier to maintain a stable pH value. Moreover, other water chemistry parameters can all be manipulated more effectively via a (usually much larger) central filtration unit. For instance, we can add several different filter media, such as peat moss, peat granulate, activated charcoal or other filter media. This is all much more difficult when dealing with smaller, individual tanks.

Above: The exemplary discus breeding facility of Werner Colle, which is serviced by a central filter. The breeding tanks are along the upper tier; all have sight barriers and they are isolated. Below are the rearing or grow-out tanks for sub-adult discus (future brood stock), respectively. The water temperature in these tanks is maintained by the central room heating system, which keeps the humidity level down since tank temperature and room temperature are nearly identical. The actual heating of the tanks is done in the central filter via a heat exchanger.

One disadvantage of operating a central filter jointly for several tanks is the possibility of transmitting diseases from one tank to another. Therefore an adequate quarantine period for newly arrived discus must always be adhered to.

The clustering of breeding tanks into groups around two or three central filter circuits seems like an excellent compromise. Depending on the size of the breeding facility, several tanks are connected to a central filter. Should a disease problem occur in one group of tanks it remains confined to those tanks and is not spread throughout the entire facility, because the other tank groups are operated on separate filter circuits.

Central filters are commonly placed below the tanks. In this case one can take advantage of gravity-flow via an overflow arrangement. Those tanks which are directly above the filter have a hole drilled into one side (done by most glazing companies). The diameter of this hole should, of course, match commercially available PVC fittings, which are then simply threaded (or glued) through or into the hole. Suitable diameter PVC pipes are then fitted to the hole, connecting each tank to the filter below. It does not need to be specifically pointed out, that several tanks can be inter-connected via 'T' and 'cross' fittings. This way the entire water volume to be filtered flows via PVC pipes into the central filter below. The filtered water, which accumulates in the 'clean' chamber is returned to the tanks above via a suitably powerful circulating pump. The water supplied to the

individual tanks are fitted with ball valves, so that the water flow into each tank can be closely controlled. Accordingly, the equivalent volume of in-flowing water is 'pushed' out of the tank through the overflow and flows back into the filter below. This closed filter system is very convenient and saves time keeping the tanks clean.

Several separate filter chambers need to be installed

Typical discus breeding tank with an average water volume of 100 litres. The fish are unable to see in to the adjacent tank since the side glass panels have been painted over with a dispersion paint. This enables the fish to concentrate on their own spawning activity and so they are not distracted by other discus. The eggs are protected against predation from the pair, through the placement of a stainless-steel mesh around the entire spawning cone. To assure maximum oxygen supply, an air stone is added, since the parents are prevented from efficiently fanning the eggs due to the wire screen.

in the filter container. The first chamber, which receives all incoming water (to be filtered), also acts as a pre-filter. Here we suspend a strainer container filter wool or a suitably large piece of foam rubber. This facilitates daily removal of all coarse debris and other dirt particles by simply rinsing the filter medium out under running water. Depending upon individual preferences, three or four other filter chambers are then added. In- and outflows (from chamber to chamber) must be arranged alternately so that all incoming water flows evenly through all filter chambers. It is advisable to place some easily washable filter medium in the first filter chamber.

In time a considerable amount of dirt will accumulate, particularly in the first chamber. This way it is easy to clean the filter medium more frequently. The second and third filter chambers are then filled with a long-term filter medium, which can easily remain several months in the filter. The last chamber with the pump is designed as a 'clean chamber', where all the filtered water accumulates before it is returned to the respective tanks via a circulating pump.

There is no categorical answer to the question as to which is the most suitable filter medium. Filter wool and artificial sponge-material have proven to be most effective. The blue artificial sponges now available through the aquarium trade are very popular, especially since they come in different porosities (densities). Moreover, they can be cleaned easily and thor-

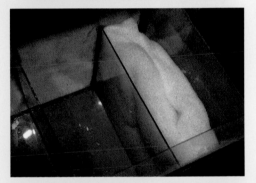

Left: A view into a central bio-filter installed at a large discus breeding facility. The incoming water (on the right) is passed through a pre-filter, which is cleaned daily. Foam mats of different densities are popular for use in bio filters. Here we find five different foam mats placed side-by-side. The filtered (clean) water is returned to the tanks via a circulating pump. This type of filtration has become very popular among discus hobbyists.

Below: A simple outside filter with filter wool. For this type of filter to function properly, additional media have to be added (apart from wool). Suitable filter media are foam rubber mats, small pieces of clay pipes, lava gravel or similar (inert) materials.

A powerful circulating pump is placed inside the clear chamber, which then returns the water to the tanks. If several tanks are serviced by this filter a water supply circuit is installed using a pipe reticulation system and valves, as required.

oughly. The long-term filter chambers can be filled with various filter media such as plastic sponges, plastic balls, lava gravel, small clay tubes or small sintered glass tubes. The use of activated charcoal is only advisable in the first chamber, and even then only when really required. Activated charcoal loses its effectiveness quickly. It is an ideal filter medium to remove residual medication, but it should not be used on a long-term basis. Similarly, the use of peat moss or peat granulate in the first filter chamber should also be of limited duration only. This way the quality of aquarium water can easily be manipulated through the use of specific filter media in the first filter chamber. For instance, if you wish to lower the pH value and add humic substances to the aquarium water, you simply place a suitable amount of peat moss (wrapped in a woman's stocking) into the first filter chamber. When after a few days the peat moss has served its purpose, it can easily be removed.

Within a central filtration circuit it is also possible to isolate an individual tank, simply by turning off the respective supply ball valve. Of course, you then will have to supply alternate filtration to the isolated tank. For instance, if a tank needs to be treated with medication, it is simply isolated from the central filter and then re-connected after a few days. Isolation of a tank may also become necessary, if you need to treat newly laid eggs with a fungicide. There are many possibilities to operate such a breeding facility on an individual basis, to accommodate your personal needs.

THE CORRECT WATER

The correct discus water is really only available at relatively few locations because municipal water suppliers always adjust the water chemistry so that the pH of tap water remains at least at pH 7.0 or above. A pH value of 7.0 is not very favorable for discus breeding, although these fish can readily be kept in such water. Moreover, most tap water is usually medium hard or even hard which is another great disadvantage for discus. Consequently, many discus hobbyists face the problem of having to recondition tap water before using it in discus tanks. Lowering the pH is the lesser of the problems involved; reducing water hardness is more difficult. If the total hardness is below 10 degrees (German) total hardness, the water can be partially softened by using peat

moss. The so-called peat moss filtration is the simplest procedure available to soften water. The light brown, so-called white peat from high altitudes is the best for this purposes. Not only does it reduce water hardness, but also adds humic acids to the water. Unfortunately, the important humic and fulvic acids from the waters of the Amazon are not available to us, and so peat moss is only a substitute of limited usefulness. Liquid peat supplements can also only approximate the natural acid capacities of native discus rivers.

The water for breeding discus needs to be suitably

conditioned before it can be used. Up to now, the standard method for softening aquarium water has been the use of ion exchangers. A partial de-ionization of water is accomplished by passing it through a cation exchanger. This is recommended when there is a high carbonate hardness in the water. You can test for hardness of your water by means of drop reagents or a conductivity meter. During the desalination (de-ionization) process water

Here a small volume of water is constantly passed over a nitrate filter (filled with ion-exchange resin) via a by-pass system. Aquarium water also flows over a slow, bio filter (blue bio balls in a column).

passes over exchange resins which facilitate a constant exchange of ions. Resins with an indicator color are most useful, such as LEWATIT S 100 G 1. With an advancing loss in ion-exchange capacity, the color of this resin changes from light brown to red. This then shows you quickly and easily when the resin needs to be regenerated, as the water to be conditioned flows slowly through this ion-exchanger and emerges at the other end as partially softened water.

Unfortunately, these resins must be regenerated from time to time; this is very much like recharging. One quart of LEWATIT S 100 or S 100 G1 requires 2 gallons of 10% hydrochloric acid. This acid must run very slowly through the resin; in fact, for 2 quarts acid we need to plan 20 minutes of regeneration time. Of course, the regenerated resin must be rinsed with at least 10 quarts of tap water before it can be used. This rinsing step should take no less than 30 minutes.

Tap water can also be completely desalinated, whereby the water runs first through a strongly acidic cation exchanger which has been loaded with hydrogen ions. This exchanger replaces all cations with H-ions and so converts all salts into their respective acids. This acidic water is then channelled through a strongly basic anion exchanger, where all anions are replaced with OH-ions. A weakly basic anion exchanger is, for instance, LEWATIT MP 62. For the regeneration of 1 quart of LEWATIT MP 62 we need 2 quarts of 3% sodium hydroxide, which must flow through the resin in not less

than 30 minutes for an effective regeneration. Subsequently, it must be rinsed with 15 quarts of tap water within 1 hour, before the resin can be used again for aquarium water. It goes without saying that the manufacturer of these resins, which are available through aquarium shops, provide specific warning leaflets for their products.

Column with exchange resin for desalinating aquarium water.

It is obvious then, that complete desalination consists of an involved exchange procedure, because we need not only two exchange resins but also two containers. The acquisition and operating costs are not exactly low, but the great advantage of complete desalination is the supply of virtually salt-free

water with extremely low conductivity. In fact, using this method we can push the conductivity down to a guide value of 5 S (Micro-Siemens). This, nearly salt-free, raw water can then be adjusted according to particular breeding requirements. That is, you can 'blend' your individual discus breeding water. It must, of course, be remembered that totally desalinated water cannot support life and therefore must not be used in an aquarium. Only after mixing it with 'normal' tap water or spring water, the desalinated water is getting some salts back and is so (re-) vitalized. Totally desalinated water can, however, be used for partial water changes or to replace evaporative water loss.

In recent years, reverse osmosis as a water conditioning procedure has become very popular among aquarists. There are now reasonably-priced units available which are not only useful for home aquarium purposes, but they have also become quite affordable. Of course, small reverse osmosis units do not make vast volumes of aquarium water, but for the aquarium hobby they are totally adequate. The nucleus of a reverse osmosis unit is a semi-permeable membrane. Since tap water contains salts and other dissolved substances, which can not penetrate the membrane, it acts like a sieve. Clean water is forced through the membrane by means of high pressure and is so separated from the dissolved substances and salt. Over-simplified, you can think of this procedure as being a method of ultra-fine filtration.

Since reverse osmosis units

for aquarium purposes work well with water (line) pressure, it is generally not necessary to use an additional motorized pump. On the other hand, the efficiency of a reverse osmosis unit is considerably enhanced through the added pressure of a pump. Since these membranes are somewhat sensitive to chlorine and dirt, it is advisable to use a pre-filter or activated charcoal filter. For further details you may wish to consult your local dealer.

The treated water from a reverse osmosis unit contains less than 10% of the (formerly) dissolved substances, and so it is almost like distilled water. As a positive side effect it is noted here that pesticide residuals are also largely removed during this process. The ratio between 'clean' water and dirty water is approximately 20% of the initial water supplied becomes desalinated for use as aquarium water. About 80% ends up being 'waste' water, and so many aquarists are reluctant to use this water conditioning method. Of course, this 'waste' water is not dirty water in the conventional sense, but perfectly good tap water, which can be used for other purposes (e.g. watering the garden).

Through the addition of further technical equipment, small facilities can gradually grow in to large professional operations, adapting to expanding demand by the discus hobbyist.

Reverse osmosis water must not be used for discus without having been mixed ('blended') with other water first. It is always advisable the increase its hardness slightly by adding tap or spring water in order to

make a viable medium for living organisms. There are now also supplements for osmosis water, which (selectively) replace some of the trace elements previously removed by the reverse osmosis process (which, incidentally, has little effect on the pH value of the original water). The pH value of water with low conductivity can be lowered quite rapidly by

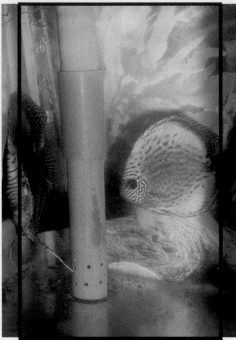

Discus require clean water for their health; you require clean water in the tank so you can see the discus and so you can maintain an odor-free discus set-up.

adding peat granulate to the filter. Generally, water with low conductivity is chemically rather unstable in regard to the pH value. Therefore, caution is advised when using peat supplements. A slow lowering or rising of the pH value presents no problems, but very sudden pH changes can cause difficulties and may even lead to fatal pH shock.

Slightly acidic water with a correspondingly low pH of 5.0 to 6.0 are ideal for breeding discus, but it needs to be stressed again that discus must not be exposed to sudden, substantial pH variations. Therefore, when transferring discus it is important to make sure that they are moved to water which has a similar pH value. Juvenile specimens react adversely of large pH variations, which can lead to irregular growth among the young.

FILTRATION FOR BREEDING TANKS

Since only a small volume of water gets replaced in a breeding tank while young discus are being reared, an effective filtration system is mandatory under these conditions. What system to use depends on various factors. Hobby breeders may have only one or two breeding tanks in operation; however, more dedicated breeders may have several tanks, possibly as many as a dozen. Clearly in each of these cases a different system needs to be used. A single tank is easy to outfit with an individually designed filtration system. Sponge filters placed inside the tank and operated with an airlift system have proven to be very suitable. This sort of filter has the advantage that it involves a slow water flow, permitting bacteria established in the sponge to initiate the reduction of nitrate. Once this sort of filter has been sufficiently conditioned (in a few days) its filtration effect is very good. When rinsing out filter sponges one should use luke-warm water, but leave some residual dirt to re-start bacterial action when the filter is recommissioned. If the filter sponge is completely washed out under flowing warm water it would totally destroy the desirable bacteria.

In some instances breeding tanks can also be operated with slow-flowing external filters fitted with suitable filter media. The filter medium used in an outside filter can influence the water chemistry. For instance, by using peat moss or peat granulate in the outside filter the pH value can be reduced slightly. On the other hand, by using filter carbon the pH can be stabilized and residual medication can be removed from the water. Slow-flowing outside filters, using sintered glass as a medium, are very useful for nitrate reduction. CAUTION: Special care must be taken with filters used in breeding tanks, so that the discus larvae are not sucked into the filter system. Consequently, filter intake pipes must be covered with a fine-meshed straining device. Discus breeders who operate several breeding tanks often incorporate all their tanks in a joint filtration circuit. Such centralized filtration has advantages as well as disadvantages. Each tank has a hole drilled (glass drill at any glazer) at the level of the surface, and PVC pipes are fitted. Via additional pipe reticulation the filtered water to be filtered is circulated through a central filter and pumped back into the individual tanks. Then the overflowing (discharge) water from these tanks is taken via pipes to the outside filter, where it is filtered and then returned to the tank. Ideally, the filter tank should be

located directly below the breeding tanks to make for short pipe runs and the use of gravity flow. The various filter chambers can be filled with filter wool, lava (volcanic) gravel, foam rubber mats, plastic balls or various granulates. Specific water supplements can also be added in these chambers. For instance, peat moss is a good filter medium to increase to acidify the pH value. With these filters it is also important to make sure that the juvenile discus are not sucked up by the intake pipes.

One advantage of these linked breeding tanks is an apparent transfer of breeding stimuli from pairs which are

spawning to other pairs not yet in a breeding mode. To that effect, I have observed repeatedly that after one pair has spawned, others will immediately commence with their breeding preparations. One disadvantage of having several tanks linked via a central filtration unit is a possible transmission of diseases; however, with healthy discus which have been sufficiently quarantined, such a danger can be excluded. Yet, the combined water volume, which — in the final analysis — is benefiting each pair, is of considerable advantage. For instance, in a facility with 6 breeding tanks the fish live essentially in

Keeping the aquarium tank bare is best for spawning discus, but it may be difficult at times since filtration in a breeding aquarium must be outfitted so it will protect the free-swimming fry.

about 400 gallons of water, while in the case of individual maintenance each pair would only be in 30 gallons. The biological equilibrium of the large water volume has a positive effect on the stability of the water and a 'crash' of water chemistry parameters is therefore avoided.

HEATING

The most widely used form of aquarium heating is the thermostatically-controlled (automatic) rod heater. Discus tanks require a water temperature of 82 - 86° F. This temperature range is easily reached and maintained with such automatic heaters. Individual tanks must therefore be equipped with such a heater. For larger facilities it is quite possible to suspend a number of automatic heaters in the central filter unit, which then provides a continuous supply of evenly heated water to all tanks. A word of caution: when suspending the

Facing Page:
Bottom left: The clutch has developed well on the sponge filter, which had not been turned off during this period. There was no danger for the larvae, since this gentle filter effect did not exert any detrimental effects on them.

Large photo:
Simple air-lift sponge filters are excellent filters for breeding tanks. They are operated individually. After a few days the sponge becomes partially blocked, which then assures an excellent filtration effect. In this tank a pair of discus has chosen the sponge filter as a spawning substrate.

As we can see, a large number of young have been raised in this tank. Although a spawning vase was present, the pair selected a totally different spawning site which did not have any adverse effects on breeding success.

heaters in the central filter it is important to make sure that all are evenly flooded by water so that there is no unnecessary (localized) heat build-up in the filter.

Large tanks or larger breeding facilities can also be heated via the central heating system of an apartment or house. To do that we need to connect heat exchangers to the central heating system pipes, and these are then installed in large filter chambers. This sort of 'central heating' is, however, only economically feasible for larger tanks or public aquarium facilities. Temperature of the aquarium water plays a large role in the time required for discus eggs to hatch.

Above and Below: This tank was filtered by means of a foam cartridge filter for the first few days after the larvae had hatched. When using central filtration it is very important to properly screen the intake so that the young fish are not sucked into the filter. Many small discus have been sucked up by such filters and many aquarist have stood in front of their tank the next morning to notice in total disbelief that all of the young discus have disappeared into the filter.

Right: Aquarium water is heated via this heat exchange pump. For large tanks or comprehensive facilities central heating can be very cost-effective.

FOR THE ADVANCED DISCUS HOBBYIST: BREEDING TECHNIQUES

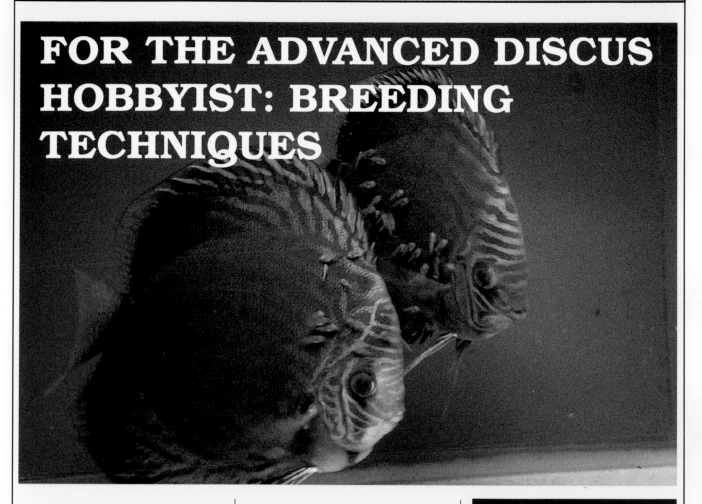

SELECTING BROOD STOCK

A perfectly matched breeding pair of discus makes for little work and few worries. Unfortunately though, one rarely ever has the luck to find such a perfect pair very easily. What does it take to get discus pair in the first place? One can either raise a group of young discus until they reach sexual maturity or buy several adult discus or — better yet — a pair of discus.

Raising young discus to a size that is ready to breed takes about 12 to 15 months. Complete rearing of young discus is not that simple and must not be underestimated. If you make the long-term commitment to raise your own discus, then you should start

with several, because discus kept in an aquarium tend to be a schooling fish. Ideally one should raise 10 to 20 small discus in a community tank. Of course, this requires an aquarium size of at least 30 gallons at the beginning. Then, at the age of 8 to 10 months this discus school should be transferred to a larger tank or the fish should be split up into separate tanks.

Another possibility — as already mentioned above — is to purchase adult discus. The advantage of this is, of course, that you can already see the genetic material of your future brood stock; however, the sexes are very difficult to determine, even in adult

The perfect discus pair guards its young in total harmony. Both adults produce a skin secretion fed upon by the young. Well adjusted pairs regularly alternate feeding their young without fighting.

discus. Most discus breeders rely on their intuition when selecting and matching the partners for breeding pairs. Any random selection of breeding pairs must, of course, be preceded by an extended observation period. Often the behaviour of adult discus within a school can provide clues of their particular sex. If fish are paired off at random they should be given a period of at least 4 to 6 weeks to mate. Once a pair of discus has spawned the adults should not be separated again, since these magnificent cichlids tend to remain bonded for long periods of time. Among adults the sexes can be determined relatively easily, since males are generally larger and the body appears stouter than that of females of the same age. Especially in the head region there are significant differences between males and females. When viewed from the front, the head in males is significantly stronger and when viewed laterally it is rounder than that of females. In females the head is more pointed when viewed from one side. Often the margins of the fins are used for sexing discus. In males dorsal- and anal fins are more drawn out than those in females. Similarly, the caudal fin in males appears somewhat wider than in females; however, these fin characteristics are not always reliable for determining the sexes. These are only indicators which can quickly go up in smoke when dealing with discus from different populations and different ages. One possibility for sexing older discus is by taking a close look at the genital papillae. To do that you have to catch the fish, hold it in a glove-covered hand and turn it upside-down. The papillae in females is distinctly larger then the genital opening of males; however, assessing these differences takes some experience. Once females have spawned several times, their papillae appear distinctly enlarged and slightly frayed. This, however, is really only visible with practice and by using a magnifying glass.

Sexing smaller discus is impossible, but the fact that males (within a sibling group, i.e. all fish of the same age) are generally larger than females, seems to generally hold true. In fact, hobbyists who may buy a small school of, say, 10 young discus and then select only the largest fish at the dealer, often find out (much later, of course) that they have raised a group of all males. Moreover, it appears that males among discus are indeed in the majority, because breeders often notice that they end up with an excess of adult males.

Sexing wild-caught discus is even more difficult than their captive progeny. An aid for determining the sex of a wild-caught fish is to turn it over and then closely examine its genital papillae. The age of these fish is indeterminable, and the finnage is the same in both sexes. Also wild-caught discus generally do not reach the size of captive-bred fishes. Over the years a dedicated discus hobbyist will get a feel for sexing discus, but even then there may still be surprises.

PREPARATIONS FOR BREEDING DISCUS

As a rule, the breeding pair is transferred to their own breeding tank, so that they can start their spawning preparations. Such a sudden change in tank environment can lead to temporary behavioral disturbances. This means that the pair may not commence spawning preparations right away. After a short period everything should return to normal and the two fish will commence breeding. The reproductive cycle of discus can be triggered by changes in water chemistry; for instance, a partial water change always has a beneficial effect on the spawning behavior of these fish. Large partial water changes cause sudden, temporary changes in the breeding water which triggers certain impulses in the breeding pair. The fish will also react to pH changes. A partial water change can, for instances, reduce the pH of the breeding water, which can have an immediate effect on the fish. Similarly, a reduction in nitrate level can also have a positive effect on the fish. Since there is a continuously rising nitrate level due to the accumulation of waste products and left-over food in an aquarium, a reduction of this from a partial water change with nitrate-free water

Opposite Page:
Above: Raising young discus at the same growth rate is not easy. Repeated, specific feedings several times a day, apart from optimal water quality maintenance are prerequisites for normal growth. If the young stop feeding, even for only a few days due to disease problems, their growth becomes impaired, which is very difficult to make up later on. The hobbyist must closely monitor the young if he wants to achieve satisfactory breeding results.

Below: A mature pair can be relatively easily culled from a group of (sibling) discus reared together in the same tank. The sex can be determined with some certainty from the behavior of the fish. It is also conspicuous that among discus kept in larger groups there is less aggression than in smaller groups of 2 to 5 specimens. In large groups, all fish have even access to food, assuring an adequate food distribution.

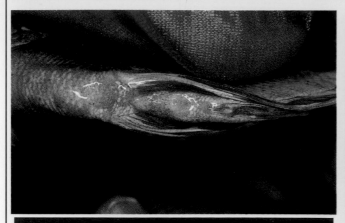

On this female we can see that the genital opening is larger than in males. This female had only spawned twice by the time this photo was taken. With increasing age and subsequent spawnings the spawning papillae becomes distinctly larger.

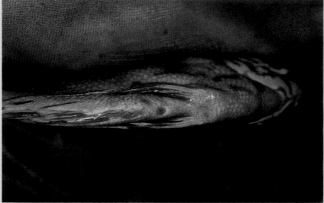

Only by placing the fish on its back and thoroughly examining the genital opening can the sex be determined, but only with some practice. Females which have spawned already a few times possess a distinctly larger, slightly frayed genital papillae. This photograph shows a male which has reached the proud size of 8 inches, yet the genital opening is relatively small. Males have the smaller genital opening compared to females.

can have a positive effect. This may also induce the fish to spawn. The use of peat moss or peat granulate can also bring surprisingly good breeding results. Peat moss, for instance, can be tied into a nylon stocking, which is then placed into the filter circuit. Alternately, the water used for partial water changes could have previously already been enriched with peat moss. To do that we fill an unused tank or plastic container with water a few days before the anticipated water change of the aquarium. The pH of the water in this reservoir can be adjusted as required, by using peat moss. The water quality of municipal water in population centers and large cities leaves — more and more — much to be desired. The water contains not only chlorine, but also nitrate and other residuals. Often there are mortalities or diseases among discus after a change of this water. In order to avoid this, the water to be used for a water change can first be filtered over activated charcoal. It is quite feasible to filter the entire reserve water for a few days over activated charcoal and then condition it with peat moss.

In Southeast Asia discus breeders produce, very successfully, large numbers of discus. One of the secrets of Southeast Asian discus production is the daily water change. This provides a continuous stimulus for breeding pairs. Similarly, growth of juveniles is positively affected by these water changes. Overall, correct water is the key to successful discus breeding.

BREEDING

The crowning achievement of any freshwater aquarist is breeding discus successfully. There is no mistaking once two adult discus have come together as a bonded pair and commenced spawning preparations. Both fish employ fin displays while swimming towards and around each other. They will 'bow', and sometimes the male pushes slightly into one side of the female. This courtship display proceeds peacefully and there is generally no danger for either of the two fish. At that point there are external changes taking place in both fish. As spawning preparations advance, both fish will change their coloration, turning rather dark, almost black, especially towards the posterior half of the body. The last four or five (of the nine) vertical bands turn solidly black. This indicates spawning is imminent. The pair looks for a suitable spawning site. Generally this is the spawning pot or cone, positioned in the center of the bottom. If it is absent, discus will accept many substitutes. If need be, they will even deposit their eggs on the aquarium glass. Once a site has been selected, the spawning substrate will be thoroughly cleaned by both fish. This can take several hours and is accompanied by shaking (shivering) of the body. This shivering is also a very distinct sign for the onset of spawning. Discus usually spawn in the evening, in breeding tanks with a water temperature of about 85° F. The water temperature has a significant influence on the development of discus eggs. At 85° F the eggs require about 55 to 60 hours for their development. This then means, for eggs laid in the evening, the larvae will hatch on the morning of the third day. This is important for the fish, because the parents care for their brood during the entire development period. Nowadays most discus breeders provide a so-called night-light for their breeding pairs. This little lamp is kept tank lights tends to frighten the fish, possibly even causing mortalities.

When spawning is imminent, the breeding pair intensifies its cleaning activities, whereby the female is usually the more active. At that point the female becomes more restless and continues to

Sexing wild-caught discus is somewhat more difficult, especially when the fish are not yet fully grown. Only at an age of 18 to 24 months will wild-caught discus have reached their maximum size. Although sexual maturity will have been reached at an age of 12 months, the fish are not yet fully grown. Generally, males develop greater body mass; on that basis they are easier to distinguish from females; however, this characteristic is not 100% reliable so there can always be surprises in respect to sex determination when breeding discus.

on throughout the night and offers the fish the opportunity to better watch over their clutch. The aquarium trade has special cost-effective lamps and even mini-fluorescent tubes just for that purpose. They provide the breeding pair with sufficient diffuse light to guard their eggs after the main tank lighting has been turned off. A sudden turning off or on of the approach the spawning site for a 'test spawning'. She swims across the site from bottom to top, and the male now begins to show interest in her. There are various reasons for the hobbyist to provide additional support at that point of the breeding activities. Sight barriers, which are between adjoining tanks, have proven to be very effective. This way individual pairs can no longer see each other in adjacent tanks. Installing the sight barrier just before or during spawning is most helpful, because some males are easily distracted and will then no longer fertilize the eggs properly.

Once the female commences laying the first egg chain or strand, it is particularly important for the male to commence fertilizing the eggs. Sperm is viable only for about 30 seconds and within that time frame a sperm must have been able to penetrate the micropyle of the eggs. The female deposits the eggs in such a way that this micropyle always points upward. During fertilization there must not be a strong current in the aquarium because this could have a

detrimental influence on the sperm flow. Therefore, it is advisable to stop the filter for about an hour while spawning is in progress. The two fish are now side-by-side in front of the spawning site and alternately pass over it. Once the female has deposited an egg strand, she swims over to one side and then the male fertilizes these newly laid eggs. The male then does a semi-circle and returns to the female. Depending upon the age of the breeding pair, spawning takes about 60 to 90 minutes. During that time the female deposits 150 to 400 eggs (the average clutch consists of about 200 eggs). Very small clutches are produced when a females spawns several times in quick succession (when the eggs

have been destroyed or eaten). Discus eggs have a length of about 1.5 mm and a diameter of 1.2 mm. The filter must be turned on again as soon as the spawning has been completed. Then the two parents position themselves in front of the clutch, fanning the eggs with their pectoral fins. This is to prevent the formation of fungus on the eggs. The night-light,

It is easy to distinguish sex characteristics when comparing the partners of a known pair. In the male depicted here, which together with the female is guarding the young, the sex characteristics are not yet strongly developed. If kept alone this fish would be difficult to sex. It takes years of experience as a discus breeder to determine the sex of adult discus with some certainty.

One of the big secrets of the discus breeding success in Southeast Asia is the enormous partial water changes, which are done daily. This is a discus husbandry practice which is now widely used in all Southeast Asian countries. Generally, at least 50 to 90% of the water is changed at least once a day. These water changes are, of course, further complemented by the high (ambient) air temperatures, which eliminates expensive water heating.

mentioned above, induces the breeding pair to guard the eggs virtually around the clock. Unfortunately there are also discus which eat their own eggs. The reason for this has not yet been determined definitively. Yet, since this egg predation usually takes place only after 50 hours after spawning, it can be assumed that the eggs did not develop properly and have therefore been eaten. As mentioned before, these are only assumptions which cannot be proven. There may also be a connection between water quality and egg predation, because the adults will know very well when their brood has good survival chances.

At a water temperature of 85° F the larvae will hatch in 55 to 60 hours. As early as the end of the second day, dark nuclei are already distinctly visible in the eggs, which indicates that they have been fertilized. These eggs have developed normally. After about 55 hours definite movement is visible inside the eggs. Observations through a magnifying glass will even reveal the beating heart and tail. The larvae hatch tail first. Another 60 hours are required for the complete development to the swimming stage. The parents transfer the larvae with their wildly beating tails, removing them from the egg shell. The young are suspended from the spawning substrate by means of an adhesive thread attached to their head. They can only move away from the substrate once their development is complete and the adhesive glands cease functioning. At that point the young will start to swim away from the substrate, only to be gathered up again by their parents in their mouth. These individual 'escapees' are gently 'chewed' and are then spat into the school of (remaining) larvae.

Above: The discus pair has selected its spawning site and decided on the vase. If such a spawning vase is available in the breeding tank it is generally selected as a spawning site.

Below: Soon the discus pair will start cleaning the spawning substrate. Both fish clean the site with their mouths and so remove algae and micro-organisms.

Below: Finally egg strands are deposited. The female approaches the spawning cone from below, and deposits the eggs during a pass, from the lower portion of the cone towards its peak. An egg strand consists of 10 to 20 eggs, on the average. The eggs are adhesive and will stick readily to the smooth substrate.

Above: The female practices spawning prior to actually depositing her eggs. This apparent 'site assessment' of the spawning pot is part of the overall breeding ritual. At that point the male will become very interested in the female and spawning is imminent. Therefore, discus breeders install sight barrier at the aquarium in time, so that there is no visual contact to the adjacent aquarium. Unfortunately, some males tend to be distracted while spawning is in progress.

Below Left: Immediately after the eggs have been laid the males fertilizes them with his sperm. It is important at that point, that there is no strong current in the aquarium, and so filter flow should be reduced or turned off.

Right: Because of the synchronized spawning movements, the pair keeps meeting at the spawning cone, where the female deposits a strand of eggs which is immediately fertilized by the male. The entire spawning process takes about an hour. It is over when the partners position themselves alternately in front of the clutch fanning the eggs, so that they get sufficient oxygen.

This female assesses the spawning pot, as the future spawning site. In doing so, she swims, in an upward pass, from below towards the peak of the cone. This type of spawning pot has proven to be ideal for breeding discus. Because of its shape it assures that the clutch is concentrated within a small area.

Hobbyists new to breeding discus tend to get somewhat nervous at this sight, and may think that this is the end of their breeding success because the parents appear to be eating the young; however, this procedure is totally harmless and nothing happens to the small larvae.

Gathering up the larvae is quite normal and as such it is part of the brood care of these cichlids. We know similar types of behavior from other cichlids. The parents need

only to be fed once daily during this period of intensive brood care. It is important though that one parent always guards the young while other is feeding.

It takes about 6 days from spawning to free-swimming larvae. From the 6th day onward, the larvae show an increased tendency of wanting to swim away from the spawning substrate. Sooner or later the parents can no longer prevent this and at that point it is extremely important that the young swim towards their parents and immediately start feeding on the nutrient cells along the surface skin of their parents. It is critically important that young find their parents without delay. The trigger for this 'swimming-towards-the-parents' is probably their dark coloration.

For that reason it is also advisable not to have dark or black objects in the tank, because this could mislead the young. It frequently happens that discus larvae swim towards dark filter sponges instead to their parents.

One should be able to assume that in a small aquarium this swimming-towards-the-parents is no problem; yet, it is a difficult situation and the parents constantly give off signs with their body, by strong, brief 'twitching' motions. If the young swim correctly to their parents, and if there are sufficient quantities of nutrient cells, the young will immediately start 'grazing' along the skin. The young discus virtually feed on the skin of their parents. This form of bonding to the parents is rather rare in the fish world. If the young have been successfully induced to 'graze' off their parents, breeding success is almost at hand. Unfortunately though there are often disruptions to this vital phase, which can be contributed to unfavorable water conditions. Problems of this nature must be due to the water, because in Southeast Asia they are hardly known. Also, our water here in Europe may be bacteriologically clean due to additives like chlorine, but in terms of trace elements present it can probably no longer be used for breeding discus without further conditioning. Consequently, if

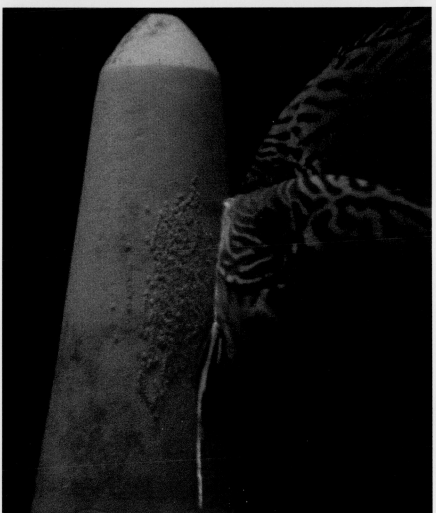

Top and bottom: This discus pair is also in harmony, spawning on a clay pot. An average clutch of discus eggs consists of about 200 eggs. The number of eggs is also dependent upon on the diet of the females as well as on the time between successive spawnings. Photos: Declercq.

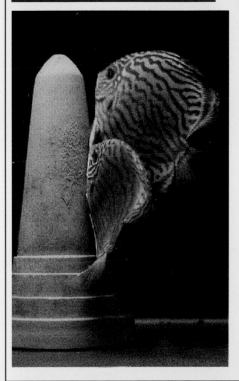

these sorts of breeding problems occur, the water quality needs to be improved before continuing on with discus breeding attempts.

The nutrient cells along the outside of the parent's skin are absolutely vital as principal food for the larvae during the first four or five days. A good sign for an adequate development of nutrient cells along the skin surface of the parents is the intense, dark color of the fish and the presence of greyish mucus, when viewed under lateral light. If this vital brood prerequisite fails, the larvae cannot survive. The development of sufficient

amounts of nutrient mucus is probably influenced by water quality. This skin secretion contains bacteria and algae, which serve as initial food for the discus larvae. It also provides the young discus with other important nutrients, such as carbohydrates, fats and proteins. It strengthens the immune system of the larvae, and as such it is absolutely vital for the young fish. Feeding on this nutrient secretion is actually what gets the digestive system of the larvae started. Four to five days after the young discus start to swim about they are also capable of feeding on

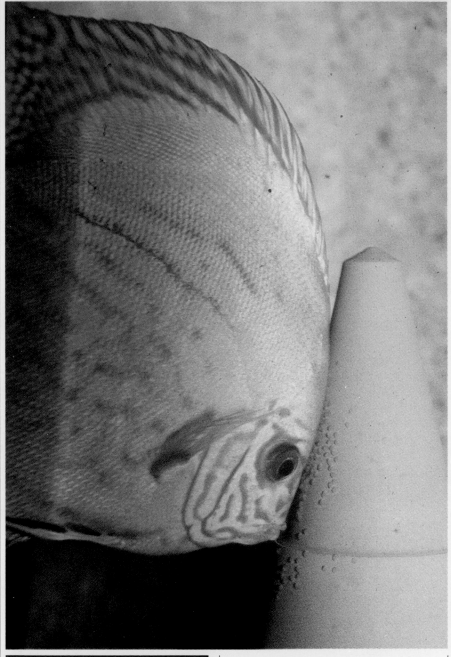

Fanning the clutch is an important part of brood behavior. This simultaneous guarding and oxygenating the eggs plays an important part in brood care. This way the breeding pair establishes a relationship to their clutch and will then later provide dedicated care for their young. The fanning is also to prevent the eggs from getting covered by fungus due to an oxygen deficiency.

week after they have started to swim about, so that parasites are not transferred from the parents to the young. Other breeders insist that the young fish must remain two to four weeks with their parents in order to guarantee access to the important parental skin secretion as a supplementary food supply. If the parents are healthy, they are not likely to transmit diseases to their young, and they can continue to profit from the nutritional value of the skin secretion.

During the first few days after free-swimming has commenced, the small discus still remain in the proximity of their parents. For that reason, supplementary food such as brine shrimp should be 'blown' into the vicinity of the young, using a thin hose. Within eight to ten days the young discus — which by then are gradually taking on the discus shape — will also feed on daphnia. This food supplement should be given four to six times daily. If, however, the young discus are being raised without their parents, they need to be fed more often. Under these circumstances it is advisable to feed the young up to ten times per day, whereby it is important that excess (left-over) food is removed regularly. After 12 to 14 days the small discus will also accept other chopped substitute foods, which can include chopped turkey heart enriched with vitamins, mixtures of vegetables and prepared food tablets, as well as chopped discus pellets.

With an adequate food supply, the small fish gradually change their shape, and the first discus shape

newly hatched brine shrimp. These tiny crustaceans are the most important, first replacement food. Once the young discus take this food they can be separated from their parents. There is some debate among discus breeders as to how long the young should remain with their parents to feed on the skin secretion. Some believe young discus can be separated one

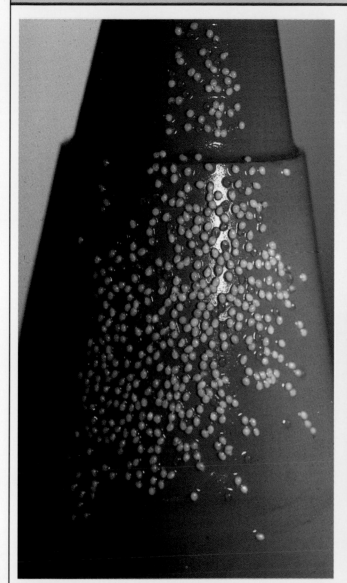

becomes visible after about 12 days. If the small discus are separated from their parents, they are best accommodated initially in small tanks, where their development can be monitored closely. Proper water maintenance is, of course, more difficult in small tanks, so it must be done meticulously. Daily removal (siphoning) of left-over food is absolutely essential, which also facilitates a partial water change. This has beneficial effects in terms of more rapid growth of the small discus.

Once they have reached the size of a quarter they can be transferred to a larger rearing (grow-out) tank. It should be noted here that the first 8 weeks in the life of young discus are important for the subsequent development of quality in these fish. Mistakes made during the first eight weeks are later almost impossible to correct. If the small discus are not feeding for a few days because of a disease, this has a rapid effect on their body shape. Water and food are the two pillars for

Covering a clutch of discus eggs with wire mesh for protection was first done in Southeast Asia. This method has also become very popular among our discus breeders. Nevertheless, one should give the discus pair an opportunity to raise their young naturally. Only after a pair has eaten their eggs several times should this protective egg guard be used.

Small catfish are ideal additions for discus grow-out tanks, because they feed on left-over food and so keep the tank clean. But they have no place in a discus breeding tank, because no matter how closely the parents guard their eggs and larvae, sooner or later the nocturnal catfish will get to them.

Above: This discus is actually covered with larvae, which feed on its skin secretion, by grazing along the skin of their parents. Discus larvae have strong bonds to their parents; they cannot survive very well without this secretion.If, after the larvae have become free-swimming, they do not immediately approach their parents, they swim aimlessly through the tank and usually die within 24 hours. It is assumed that at the point of free-swimming the larvae respond to the dark coloration of their parents. Therefore, it is advisable not to have any other dark objects in the tank, which could confuse the larvae.

Below: Usually the discus pair will deposit its eggs on the back of a spawning pot (opposite the side facing the front of the aquarium). In this case the spawning pot with newly hatched larvae was gently turned around for photography purposes, to show that the larvae are still firmly attached to the spawning substrate. Some breeders actually remove the pots together with the clutch or newly hatched larvae, to have them reared by another pair. This way two clutches can be reared simultaneously by a pair with good brood care characteristics. Professional breeders use this method of 'foster-rearing' to produce large numbers of discus progeny.

perfect discus development and subsequent breeding success. At the age of eight weeks the young discus are about 2 inches long from tip of snout to tip of tail. Many breeders will then start selling them at that point.

Discus come from the rivers of Amazonia, which carry water largely devoid of fish pathogens. In our home aquaria we can not really offer this sort of germ-free environment, because a small aquarium can never replace the vast water volumes of the rivers. Consequently, keeping discus in an aquarium is

Right: This portrait picture shows how the larvae are scattered around the entire body of the parent in order to feed on the skin secretion.

Below: In the foreground of this picture the distinctly larger male has all the larvae attached to his skin. Discus pairs with proper brood care characteristics normally take turns in leading and feeding the larvae with their skin secretion.

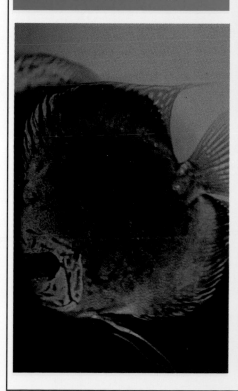

Above: Brine shrimp can easily be hatched from eggs available from most aquarium shops. To do that we add one to two teaspoons of brine shrimp eggs to a bottle filled with saltwater (one heaping tablespoon of sea salt per quart of water). With adequate aeration, illumination and oxygen supply the tiny shrimp (nauplii) hatch within 24 hours. They can be sifted out with special sieves (also available from aquarium shops), and are then fed directly to the young discus. Complete brine shrimp hatching kits are available from aquarium shops.

Right and Facing Page: This discus pair is leading a large number of young, which are already taking supplementary food. But bonding to the parents remains strong, so that in the event of danger the young will gather closely around their parents.

Properly guarding pairs do not fight over who is to lead the young; instead they alternate in this task. The fish on the left is currently leading the young, and all of the young follow the parent in a tight school behind the cone.

At this point all the young are still gathered around the parent on the left. The parent on the right is about to take over and indicates this by 'twitching' movements.

Gradually the young are changed over to the other parent.

The change-over is nearly complete, and many of the young are gathered around the parent at the right, and start grazing on the skin secretion.

Here too the change over from one parent to the other takes place without any problems. The young have no problems with this ideal breeding pair in selecting suitable feeding sites. There is no aggression between the parental partners, who guard their young jointly and with great dedication. The female on the right is distinctly smaller than the male, which clearly shows the typical sex characteristics.

Discus larvae must be protected from the filter intake, otherwise there is the danger that they will get sucked into the filter system where they will die. In this photograph the breeder has covered the intake pipe temporarily with filter wool.

This discus male leads its brood through the aquarium. Sometimes it can happen that if parents become upset they will eat their young, even when these are already 8 days old. Normally the pair will then immediately spawn again. Why this sort of parental predation happens is not known.

Left: If the small discus are separated from their parents very early, it is difficult to rear them with a suitable replacement diet. Cyclops and daphnia are suitable as food, apart from brine shrimp. Some manufacturers offer liquid foods, which, however, are insufficient by themselves as sole rearing food.

always an improvisation and means dealing in compromises. For the successful husbandry and especially for breeding discus, germ-free water is an important prerequisite. Once the water quality parameters are optimal and conform largely to those in nature, then the stress on the discus kept under these conditions is reduced. When the fish are exposed to less stress, there are also fewer complications during breeding. For that reason, some breeders keep their breeding stock in large tanks, because it reduces the element of stress encountered in small tanks. If a breeding tank covers an area of only 20 x 20 inches the two fish have to get along within a substantially reduced space. During spawning preparation and after spawning, the pair is continuously exposed to stress situations. The outcome

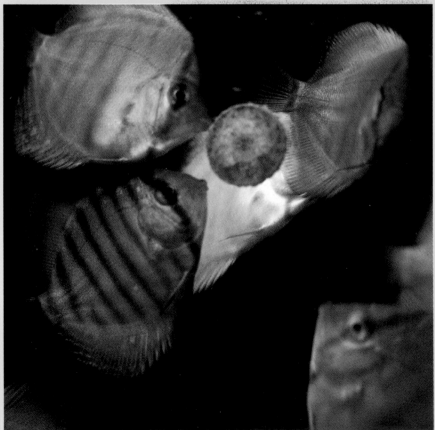

Left: Small discus are also keen to feed on food tablets, which can be given to them from the 14th day onward. These tablets can be fortified by soaking in a liquid vitamins in order to assure optimal vitamin supply to the young. Ground up flake foods, pellets and other ready-made foods can also be offered to the young. If the breeder takes his time, he will find that discus will accept all substitute foods after a period of adjustment.

The young are densely crowding around the male in the twilight of the aquarium. It is advisable to keep a small night light burning above the tank so that small discus do not become disoriented when the tank lights are suddenly turned off and they lose contact with their parents.

Unusual behavior patterns sometimes emerge when discus select a spawning site. This pair, in a community tank, have decided to attach their clutch to a piece of bamboo.

Full female ready for spawning. Sometimes a female will lay eggs with another female's assistance.

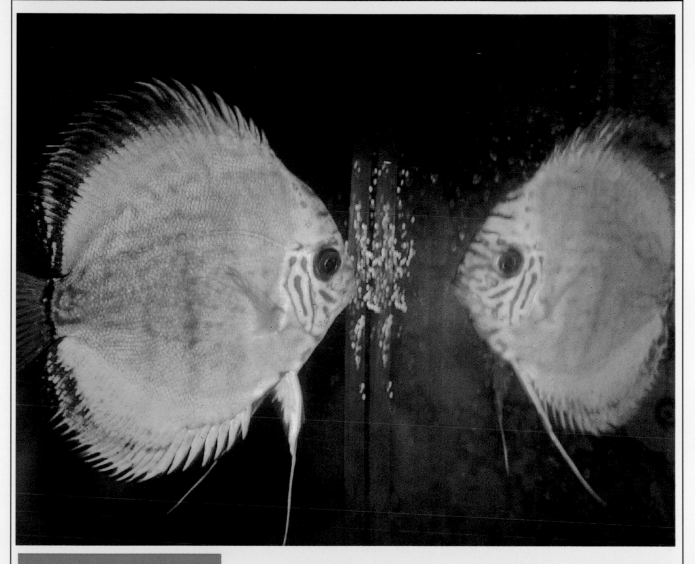

This female has deposited her eggs to one of the glass sides of the tank. In Southeast Asia some discus breeders do not provide their fish with any substrates, an so the fish have to use the glass walls. There are no distinct advantages for the breeder using this method; why it is done remains unknown.

of such a stressful situation can result in the fish eating their own eggs or even the larvae that have already hatched or are already free-swimming. Such deviant behavior can possibly be reduced by using larger breeding tanks, but this is only an assumption that has not yet been proven to be correct. It stands to reason, however, that discus pairs kept in 30 gallon tanks have more possibilities to stay out of each others way. It should be worth at least a try to transfer a pair which is known to eat its own eggs, into a

larger tank, in order to test this assumption.

A stress situation which affects a particular breeding pair of discus, must certainly also prevent optimal development of mucous secretion. It is a common complaint among discus breeders, that their breeding pairs do not develop sufficient secretion or none at all. Reducing the effects of stress on the fish may be able to eliminate this problem.

In small breeding tanks it is easier to hand-feed the young discus directly. In large tanks the food tends to spread out, and initially the young do not stray far from their parents, and so some of the food may float out of their reach.

DISCUS NUTRITION: VITAL INFORMATION FOR THE HOBBYIST

Even large discus can be changed over to nearly any substitute food. The prerequisite is, however, that the breeder really looks after his fish and takes his time feeding them. New types of food should always be offered first thing in the morning. At that time they are at their hungriest and will then readily accept new types of food.

Discus tend to learn quickly how to get at the food. These discus feed aggressively on frozen food, which of course thaws out quickly in the warm tank water. Part of successful discus breeding lies in a varied diet for the young. A one-sided diet does not provide for optimal development.

Genetic characteristics, such as color, sex and size are handed out by nature. Factors such as growth and — ultimately — size can be substantially affected by the composition of the diet. With a one-sided or inadequate diet, discus would quickly sustain deficiencies in their condition which would clearly manifest themselves. Therefore, discus in captivity must be given a variable and nutritious diet. In the wild, discus feed on freshwater shrimp, insect larvae, algae, but also on the seeds of fruit. Small freshwater shrimp play a particularly important role in the diet of discus in the wild. These shrimp contain algae and other plant material, which proves that vegetable matter is an important constituent in the diet of discus. Moreover, the carotenoid content of the shrimp affects the more intensive coloration of wild-caught discus than can be accomplished in captive-bred fish reared on a substitute diet. The significance of carotenoids in respect to a more intensive coloration in discus has, in the meantime, also been recognized by fish food manufacturers. In fact, often they now fortify their foods with these substances.

Aquarists are often surprised that their fully grown discus will not feed for prolonged periods of time, without showing a distinct loss in weight. Discus, like all fish, are cold-blooded animals and therefore do not require any energy input just to maintain a specific body temperature.

In small breeding tanks it is easier to hand-feed the young discus directly. In large tanks the food tends to spread out, and initially the young do not stray far from their parents, and so some of the food may float out of their reach

Discus food pellets are also popular among breeders. After a certain period of adjustment the fish will take them eagerly. When purchasing these pellets make sure you are buying a quality brand. Only then can you be sure your fish are provided with optimal nutrition.

Moreover, they are almost neutrally buoyant in water and so little (physical) energy is required to maintain their position. For that reason discus can go for days without food. If too many nutrients are provided, there is an increased uptake of glycogen (starch in the liver) and fat in the body tissue. Such an increased food intake and storage of fats can lead to a fatty liver. If the discus are fed mainly on substitute foods, there can be a deficiency of vitamins and minerals. Amino acids are essential for normal body development in discus. Many of these essential amino acids cannot be manufactured by the body of the fish, but instead must be taken up in food. These essential amino acids are very strongly represented, for instance, in fish and crustacean flesh. If discus feed on a lot of fish or meat, they are provided — in a natural way — with a large part of essential amino acids. On the other hand, fats should not be a major dietary component for these fish, so that they do not get too fat. Far better is a diet consisting of carbohydrates, because the fish body can — if need be — convert these into fat. A major part of the carbohydrates taken in is used as an energy carrier. Carbohydrates are principally plants, such as starch and cellulose. This cellulose cannot be digested by the body and is subsequently secreted as ballast substances. Cellulose fulfills an important tasks for the digestive process.

The food of discus also contains vitamins and minerals. This means that vitamins and minerals are taken in

Feeding adults and fry at the same time often results in the adults eating the fry food (especially if it's *Artemia*). They then leave their adult food uneaten, possibly fouling up the tank or starving the fry.

automatically while feeding. Fish food made from animal products or live fish foods contain a lot of minerals and vitamins.

Food intake and digestion also influence the use of oxygen in an aquarium. Consequently when fish feed, oxygen is also being used up. Discus should not be fed for at least 24 hours before being transported, so that they can overcome the transit period without difficulties. For discus shipments over long distances the fish should ideally be starved at least for 48 hours before they are packed.

Discus are omnivorous feeders. This means that they will feed on just about anything, animal matter as well as a partly vegetarian diet. Consequently, they can be adapted to any new diet. Of course, a change in diet

always means some extra work for the hobbyist. After all, the fish are used to their particular foods. Especially when rearing young discus, one can lay the foundation for these fish accepting all types of foods later on. When small discus are 'weaned' on to different foods, they should readily accept previous foods again once they have grown up.

If you want to change your fish over to a new type of food, this should be offered early in the morning as the very first food, because then the fish are at their hungriest. Discus like to pick up their food off the bottom. Therefore, they are typical bottom feeders because in tanks with a sandy bottom they actually 'blow' in to the substrate to extract food organisms and then eat them. The size of food items is important for discus; they prefer small food items. Even adult discus will take large food items only reluctantly. They are typical 'gulpers', which means food taken in to the mouth is immediately swallowed. Actually they do not chew and therefore the odor of discus food must be acceptable to the fish and stimulate their swallowing instinct. Fish have a well-developed sense of smell and react to various olfactory agents. Color of the food is also of importance. There is an obvious preference for food which is distinctly red. Since discus nowadays hardly ever get life food, the fish do not react to any movements by the food. This then means that it is not necessary to offer food which moves. It is only important for the food to sink, because food which floats at the surface is only taken reluctantly. For that reason, frozen foods strongly accommodate the feeding behavior of discus. Once thawed out, frozen food falls quickly to the bottom where it can be picked up effortlessly by discus.

Since discus actually sleep, the tank lights should be turned on at least 20 to 30 minutes prior to the first feeding. Only then will discus become active and start eagerly searching for food.

Experience has shown that aquarium fish are often overfed, although most aquarists tend to deny this. After all, the fish are feeding very aggressively and therefore it is assumed that they must be feeling well; however, because of an incorrect or one-sided diet a fatty liver or other damage can occur in fish quickly, which often do not

Healthy, heavy-bodied discus cannot be raised to maturity without a substantial diet of healthy foods. Pet shops carry a full line of good frozen foods, but stay away from frozen tubifex.

manifest themselves externally.

Frozen food is becoming increasingly popular as discus food, because live foods are more and more difficult to obtain. Live food such as tubifex is already heavily contaminated with pollutants and should really not be fed to discus. Even rinsing them will not improve their dietary value. The quality of mosquito larvae varies from good to inferior. Excessive feeding with mosquito larvae is not advisable. Feeding bloodworms is less problematic, but initially these are only taken reluctantly. An excellent frozen food for discus are adult brine shrimp. These 6 to 8 mm long shrimp are available freshly frozen. They have

a high carotene content, and when this food is offered in copious amounts the discus will get a beautiful red coloration, that is, the existing red color shades will intensify considerably.

Equally popular with discus hobbyists, as well as with their fish, are fish food pellets made by several manufacturers. Following a period of adjustment, discus readily accept them. This then is an excellent food which is always available. Of course, this must not lead to a monotonous, exclusive diet of pelletized food. As mentioned above, discus require a varied diet, because only that assures proper growth and avoids deficiency syndromes.

An example of consequent selection of particular specimens is the breeding result of crosses between brown discus and pigeon blood discus. Breeders have now succeeded for the first time to breed red discus without the aid of food dyes. These discus are being designated as marlboro discus by their breeder, Kitti from Thailand.

REARING DISCUS: GETTING THE MOST OUT OF YOUR EFFORTS

ARTIFICIAL REARING

Rearing discus artificially has been problematic to discus breeders for years. Before Jack Wattley, the well-known American discus breeder, other Americans attempted to rear discus by artificial means. They even offered the recipe for their 'secret food' for sale. A substantial sum had to be paid for a simple photo-copy of the so-called mixture. Yet, it was Jack Wattley who was probably the first discus breeder to rear large numbers of young discus without the parent pair being present. His methods are described in a book entitled *Jack Wattley's New Discus Handbook*. But Wattley also recognized the disadvantages of artificial rearing, and so nowadays even he raises a large number of his discus with the parents present. The basis for all rearing or grow-out diets has always been egg yolk or powdered egg yolk. Wattley described his recipe as a simple paste of powdered egg as used by cake bakeries. Powdered eggs mixed with water into a paste was then smeared along the edge of tanks containing the discus larvae. This enabled the larvae to feed on the egg mixture along the edge of the tank. Egg powder will quickly spoil the relatively small volume of water in a breeding tank, and so it must be changed daily, or the larvae are to be transferred to another tank. This artificial rearing procedure is very labor intensive and certainly involves other disadvantages, although these are never admitted by those in support of this rearing method. As was clearly shown, discus larvae require the nutrient cells of the parental epidermis during the first few days of their life. These nutrient cells, which are formed on the skin and are known to discus breeders as secretion or mucus, stimulate the digestive system of the larvae and also provide them with their first immune defense substances. In terms of its significance, this skin secretion can indeed be compared to mother's milk. Yet, the debate about artificially rearing discus will never be silenced. There will always be the case where a discus breeder has difficulties rearing the brood of some interesting or valuable discus strain, and like it or not, he will then resort to artificial rearing. There is supposed to be a discus farm in Indonesia, which rears discus in large numbers using artificial methods, and then dumps the fish on the market at extremely low prices. This cannot possibly be the ultimate purpose of breeding discus—producing huge numbers at low cost so that the fish can be sold very cheaply. For aquarists the more attractive way of breeding discus is certainly the natural method, that is, with the parent discus taking over the principal task of rearing the young. This method can be further improved by using planted and well-decorated, natural tanks for rearing these fish. Anyone who has ever experienced how a pair of discus has reared its young in a planted tank, will be so thrilled that he will quickly forget all about artificial rearing methods.

For the sake of completion, a recipe for the food mixture used for artificially rearing discus should be listed here.

The following ingredients are mixed together: one raw egg yolk and half of a raw egg white with one egg hard-boiled egg yolk (macerated through a strainer). Half a teaspoon of gelatine powder and half a teaspoon of agar are dissolved in .05 liters of hot water, which is then mixed into egg mixture. So that this egg mixture retains a paste-like consistency, we mix in 1/4 teaspoon of glycerin (from a drugstore). The glycerin is to assure that the egg mixture remains suitably pliable once it is dry. This egg mixture is then applied — as a thin layer — to parchment paper or a plastic bag, which is then exposed to sunlight or placed in an oven at 150° F to dry slowly. Using a sharp razor blade, the dry egg mixture is then removed from its substrate and stored in pieces. Later, as required, small amounts of them are pasted along the edge of a rearing tank or tub, where the egg mixture gradually starts to soften again. Eventually the discus larvae will accept this food and then start to grow up slowly. Supplementary feeding with microscopically small vinegar eels is also possible. Two days after having commenced free-swimming, the young discus larvae will be able to handle them. Vinegar eels are very small and are best drained into a paper coffee filter. This filter, with the retained eels is then suspended in the discus rearing tank. Get yourself a starter culture of vinegar eels and breed them in a jar filled with apple vinegar and water at a ratio of 1:1. A bit of sugar added is sufficient as food for vinegar eels. Breeding is enhanced with slight aeration. Once you have managed to get the small discus larvae over the first five days with this first artificial rearing food, they will be able to handle live, newly-hatched brine shrimp nauplii from the fifth day onward. Opponents of this artificial rearing method believe that growth of the young discus is poor and development is generally slower. Whether this is actually so remains to be seen.

BREEDING PIGEON BLOOD DISCUS

The breeding set-up shown here is used by Ronny Nuyts for breeding the pigeon blood discus variety from Southeast Asia. This discus was first bred in Thailand; it represents a mutative strain, which now has found its way around the world. It is alleged that the pigeon blood discus is very robust and ideally suited for cross-breeding with other discus. But it is also said that the formation of skin secretion is poor, leading to problems in rearing this strain. The sequence of photographs presented here gives an

accurate account of the successful breeding of pigeon blood discus.

Below: Located below the breeding tanks are the filter chambers with gravel as a medium. Water is being conditioned for a few days in the blue barrel on the left, before it is used for partial water changes.

Above: A clay vase is available to the discus pair as a spawning substrate. The overflow stem visible on the right was surrounded with wire mesh so that the fish would not use the pipe as a spawning substrate.

Right: The pigeon blood pair guards the newly-hatched larvae. It is conspicuous how closely both parents guard their brood.

Above:
This close-up shows that the larvae are well advanced in their development and are hanging from the spawning substrate by means of the head thread. At that stage the adults start to suck up the larvae and transfer them.

Left:
The first substitute food for the larvae — 4 to 5 days after they have commenced free-swimming — is brine shrimp. Brine shrimp nauplii are newly hatched tiny shrimp, which can easily be handled by the discus larvae at that stage. Brine shrimp are hatched in sea water from eggs available from aquarium shops.

Young discus feeding aggressively on brine shrimp. In the background we see a parent, which — on the basis of its dark coloration — is still producing skin secretion.

THE WORLD SCENE: COMMERCIAL DISCUS BREEDING IN ASIA

The largest and most efficient discus production centers of the world are nowadays located in Southeast Asia. As early as 20 years ago the Asians recognized the economic importance of ornamental fish breeding. Long before discus were bred there, the area produced and exported vast numbers of other ornamental fish. Countries like Thailand, Singapore, Hong Kong, Malaysia, Philippines, and Taiwan collectively produce more than one million discus for export. In view of these numbers, one can easily appreciate the importance of these fish for the local tropical fish trade.

United States, the Asians succeeded quickly building up high quality discus brood stock. For many years they flooded the discus market with high-quality regular turquoise- and solid-colored turquoise varieties. Demand for Asian discus grew quickly and many breeders succeeded in breeding interesting color varieties. Since the Asians are

Above: Discus breeding and holding facilities can be operated in Asia quite cost-effectively, since electricity and water charges are very low. As in this facility in Thailand, up to 90% of the water is replaced daily. If this is not done regularly though, high tank population densities and the intensive feeding methods will quickly lead to massive bacteria explosions. Consequently, fish from Thailand are often affected by skin pathogens.

Facing Page: At the age of four weeks the typical pigeon blood discus coloration is already clearly visible. While these discus were incredibly expensive a few years back, their price has now become more realistic due to mass production.

In the beginning of discus breeding in Southeast Asia, little attention was paid to the quality of these fish and only production numbers mattered; however, today aspects of quality and color intensity are very important. Principal importers of Southeast Asian-bred discus are — apart from Japan and the United States — the European countries, where discus are popular aquarium fish.

Through buying up discus brood stock of excellent color qualities in Europe and the

always hunting for new discus varieties, it was unavoidable that aimless crossing attempts produced mutations, which passed on their color characteristics genetically. In Thailand this lead to the 'pigeon blood discus' and in Malaysia to the 'ghost discus'. While the latter was not a success internationally, the pigeon blood discus became popular world-wide. Since these mutated discus are rather hardy, they have become established as typical 'beginners' discus'. Large

Above: If fighting breaks out between the partners of a pair rearing young, the adults are simply separated by a coarse-mesh wire partition. The young continue to have access to both parents to feed on their skin secretion.

Below: Separating the adults is not only done in order to avoid fighting, it is also used to condition one adult to another to form a breeding pair. Once the fish have gotten used to each other and there are no signs of aggression, the 'cage' is removed and the fish are likely to get on with each other. This procedure can expedite spawning activities, because the female is no longer being chased by the male in the cage.

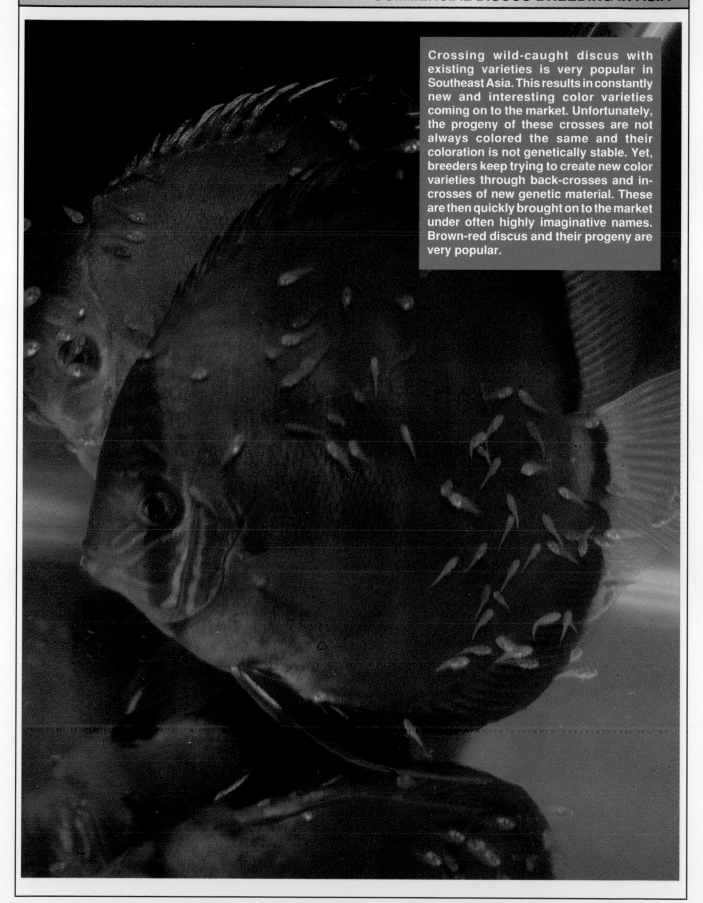

Crossing wild-caught discus with existing varieties is very popular in Southeast Asia. This results in constantly new and interesting color varieties coming on to the market. Unfortunately, the progeny of these crosses are not always colored the same and their coloration is not genetically stable. Yet, breeders keep trying to create new color varieties through back-crosses and in-crosses of new genetic material. These are then quickly brought on to the market under often highly imaginative names. Brown-red discus and their progeny are very popular.

Tubifex continues to be a very popular main food in Southeast Asia. These worms are kept in dishes under flowing water. The constant flow also cleans the worms somewhat. Nevertheless, this food is loaded with harmful substances and must not be the principal choice among foods available for discus.

numbers of pigeon blood discus are, for instance, exported to the United States.

What are the differences between Southeast Asian discus breeding and that of Europe? While discus breeding in Europe is primarily hobbyist-based, the Southeast Asians have turned discus breeding into a profession. Even if they have only a few tanks, producing only a few hundred fish per month, this is their principal job providing them with most — if not all — of their income. This sort of fish breeding is

very much facilitated by ambient tropical temperatures, which generally make heating the breeding tank unnecessary. This then eliminates a substantial cost factor and gives the Southeast Asians an advantage. Similarly, water costs in Southeast Asia compared to Europe are very low. Unfortunately the water in many areas in Europe already carries a substantial load of inorganic components, although generally still within officially-set quality parameters. On the other hand, water quality in Southeast Asia appears to be substantially better, because apparently discus eggs do not seem to get covered up by fungus as badly as in Europe. However, it is not only the better quality of water, ideal temperatures and economic locations, but also lower costs of living combined with cheap labor, which make it possible to operate even medium-size facilities very cost-effectively. Consequently, this enables the Asians to flood the market with low prices. But Asian discus are not always cheap; quite to the contrary. New strains or varieties out of Asia are often quite expensive. If a breeder is successful in producing a new color variety and manages to rear the young to a point where the color becomes visible, he will create a trade name for this discus. Then through appropriate publicity and marketing he will attempt to sell his fish at higher prices. But soon thereafter the market demand is satisfied and the price starts to come down. After that the hunt for a new variety begins and the

game starts all over again.

A substantial difference to discus breeding in Europe is the fact that the water is rarely ever filtered. Instead of water filtration, preference is given to water replacement. Since water is inexpensive and of good quality, a large volume can be exchanged on a daily basis. Most breeders change up to 90% of their aquarium water daily. Because of such enormous water changes the fish grow very well, and diseases are kept down to a minimum. Unfortunately though, in some countries it has become common practice to treat not only sick fish with antibiotics, but also use this medication as a prophylactic.

Below: Discus will spawn on virtually any object present in an aquarium. If none are present they will, out of necessity, spawn on the glass. Plastic pipes serving as tank overflows are intended as spawning substrate in Hong Kong. Breeders do not provide additional clay pots or similar spawning substrates. In this photograph a female is depositing an egg strand on such an overflow pipe.

This is the principal reason why disease pathogens have become resistant against antibiotics. Therefore, in the event of a disease outbreak in our tanks, it is often difficult to find an effective medication.

A high quality diet is another factor for the large size of discus in Southeast Asia. While tubifex are still an important food in Thailand, breeders in Hong Kong feed mainly bloodworms. In Malaysia the preferred discus diet is shrimp and mosquito larvae, while Japanese breeders insist on beef heart mixtures for their fish. In Southeast Asia, discus are bred exclusively in tanks of a size range from 20 to 30 gallons volume. Each tank contains one pair, but the spawning substrate chosen depends not only on individual preferences by breeders, but it also varies from country to country. The collection of spawning substrates used ranges from classic clay cones, bricks, slate tiles, plastic pipes to

Above: Filter boxes mounted on top of aquariums are very popular in Hong Kong and Japan. This way each tank can be filtered separately. The length of these filter boxes is adjustable. Many of these filter boxes are now being imported from China, however, the quality of pumps used is very poor, so that total losses are not uncommon.

Left: This is an interesting color variety from Hong Kong, where it is traded as diamond discus. One characteristic of this variety is the absence of the vertical bands on the gills and head. These fish are indeed completely blue-green.

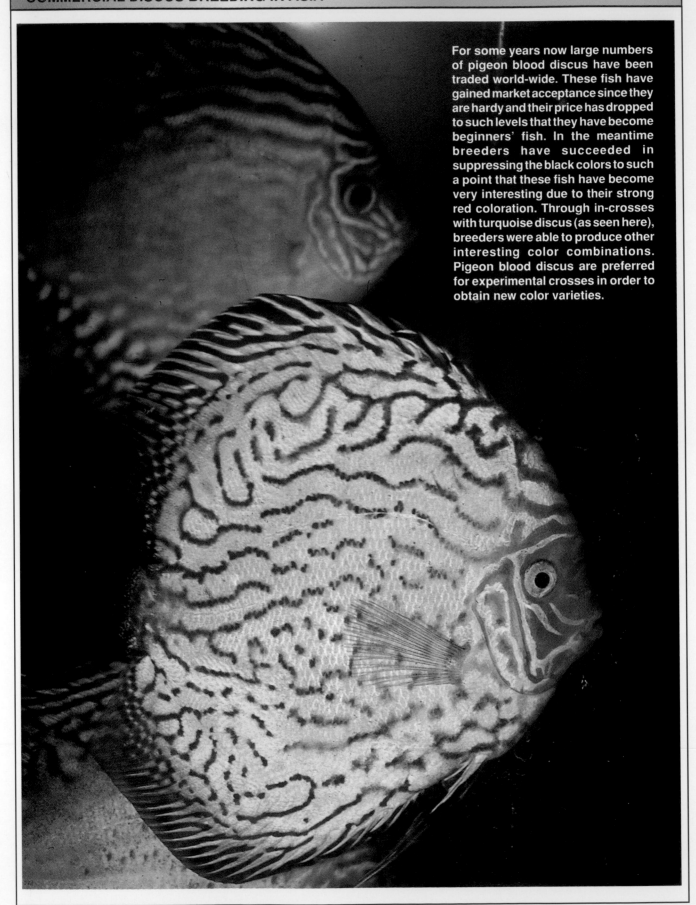

For some years now large numbers of pigeon blood discus have been traded world-wide. These fish have gained market acceptance since they are hardy and their price has dropped to such levels that they have become beginners' fish. In the meantime breeders have succeeded in suppressing the black colors to such a point that these fish have become very interesting due to their strong red coloration. Through in-crosses with turquoise discus (as seen here), breeders were able to produce other interesting color combinations. Pigeon blood discus are preferred for experimental crosses in order to obtain new color varieties.

Right: Since water is relatively inexpensive in Southeeast Asian countries and even flows warm out of the tap, breeders have changed over to permanent water changes (i.e. operating a so-called open water system). Via a water channeling system, water flows continuously into each tank and so replaces 'used' water, which is pushed out (displaced) of the tank through an overflow and into a drain. Because of the large amount of fresh water coming in to each tank, filtration is no longer required.

Below: Discus farms in Southeast Asia do not always conform to what we expect them to be. Here is an example of a very simple breeding facility, which has been set up right next to a house. Most tanks are outdoors and are partially covered with corrugated sheet metal. Although the facility appears primitive, this Malaysian breeder produces substantial numbers of high quality discus.

A current sales hit in Southeast Asia is the 'ocean green discus'. This variety has an intensive, metallic green sheen and a high body shape, which comes very close to Japanese ideals as to what a discus should look like. Fish of this quality and at a size of 2 inches can command a high price.

Above: The opposite of the simple discus breeding set-up is this modern, well-equipped breeding and holding facility of the Penang Discus Farm. Great value is placed here on cleanl presentation of the fish, because now many Japanese customers come to Penang to select their fish on site.

Below: Since large discus are also easily sold, some breeders have specialized in rearing discus to an age of one year. Only if the water quality is constantly optimized can large numbers of these fish be kept together in the same tank. In Southeast Asia this is done primarily through daily water changes.

totally bare tanks, where the fish have to spawn on the glass. A very popular method is to protect the clutch with a wire screen. Most breeders use this protective device in order to stop the breeding pairs from eating their own eggs. Even when the fish have no intention of doing that, they are still prevented from directly caring for their clutch.

Once the larvae hatch and commence free-swimming, the parents will generally raise them without any problems. If, however, arguments break out between the two partners, they are separated by a wire screen. That means the breeding tank is divided by a wire screen into two halves. Mesh size of the screen is selected so that the young can easily swim through to both parents. Often this sort of procedure becomes routine for breeders, and they will then always use it, without giving

much thought about whether these methods bring advantages or disadvantages to breeding discus.

The small discus are soon started on brine shrimp nauplii to facilitate rapid growth. Depending on individual preferences, the young are separated sooner or later from their parents and are then kept in special rearing tanks. The small discus have to grow quickly, so that they can soon be sold. At an age of about 8 weeks they will have reached a size of 2 inces and can then come onto the market. A selling size of 1 1/2 inches is very popular among dealers, because at that size the fish are cheap and find a ready market. Unfortunately, this sort of production line breeding is less than gentle on the small discus. Subsequently, they will require a lot of care and attention by their owncr if they are to grow up into magnificent specimens.

When raising discus there are always individual specimens which show interesting color or other genetic characteristics. These discus are then selected for further breeding experiments. It takes close monitoring of large numbers of adult discus to observe particular characteristics.

The growth of the discus market in Southeast Asia continues unabated. More and more discus varieties are becoming available, and in many countries there now are regular discus shows being held, where hundreds of adult specimens are exhibited. These shows broaden awareness among aquarists and so assure that the circle of discus hobbyists continues to grow.

THESE ARE TRUE SECRETS
THE SECRETS OF BREEDING DISCUS

BY JACK WATTLEY
AMERICA'S FOREMOST DISCUS BREEDER

The art and science of raising newly-hatched discus fry in an artificial manner—away from their parents—has moved to a higher level over thousands of trials in our hatchery in Florida. The procedures that we use have been refined and fine-tuned with the result that the most current information as well as our carefully-crafted formulas are now available to all discus keepers who seek greater success in raising discus fry.

We will begin on the assumption that the breeder has healthy, sexually mature discus breeding, or read to breed, with a viable sperm count in male fish, and with water and feeding procedures in order. That said, we will begin step-by-step to take you through our complete program.

SPAWNING SITE

In all probability your discus will be spawning on bricks, cones, slates or PVC in the aquarium. In our hatchery the discus would normally deposit their eggs on the overflow outlet drains, which are cemented into the bottom of the tanks. In order to remove the eggs we first had to place a removable PVC sleeve over the outlet drain. These ten-inch sleeves can easily be removed after the spawning act and placed in the hatching containers. Some sleeves stand straight up, others are on an angle, depending on where the eggs have been laid.

In some cases the female may deposit her eggs on the aquarium glass. If this is the case, all may not be lost. With a new single-edge razor blade the eggs can be carefully "shaved" off the glass sides into a clean net and placed in the hatching container with a solution of methylene blue 1%. A new single-edge razor blade will be covered with a light protective coat of oil, which must be removed prior to using. Hot water and careful wiping will ready the

Jack Wattley is not only America's foremost discus breeder and developer of new color varieties, he is also the world's leader in the artificial rearing of discus.

A pair of Wattley's discus spawning on a broad leaf. Discus might
spawn on anything solid, including the glass sides of an
aquarium. Photo courtesy of
Bernd Degen.

blade for use.

If you observe the spawning, which generally takes place in the late afternoon, it is important to ensure that the male fish has completed his fertilizing "runs" on the spawning receptacle. The complete spawning act usually takes no longer than an hour, although some spawns are completed in as little as fifteen minutes.

In the process of moving the receptacle from the aquarium to the hatching container the eggs will be exposed to the ambient air temperature of the room. (In our hatchery all aquarium water is kept at the same temperature as the room, with the exception of some of the pans that we use for the newly-hatched discus fry.) It is not necessary to worry about the eggs being out of the water during the transfer. Air exposure for ten to fifteen seconds will not hurt the eggs a bit. Recently we had a case where we were convinced that a spawn removed from the hatching container was not viable. The eggs were out of the water for at least one minute while they were examined under a magnifying glass. It was easier to place the PVC spawning receptacle with the eggs into a hatching container than to walk to the sink in another part of the hatchery to dispose of the spawn, so we did so, and the eggs hatched out in a very satisfactory manner.

HATCHING TECHNIQUES

We hatch our discus eggs in one gallon, rectangular all-glass aquariums, although not

A close up of the female actually depositing eggs as shown on the facing page. Photo courtesy of Bernd Degen.

1). The pair search for a place to deposit their eggs. Anything solid will work well for them.

all eggs are hatched artificially. Approximately sixty percent of the spawns are left with the parents, and the other forty percent are raised artificially. The hatching water is from a three-hundred gallon holding tank with a microsiemens hardness count of 250 and a pH (with the aid of Canadian peat) of 6.2-6.4. The water is initially passed through an activated carbon filter to remove chloramines that are present in the local water supply. This water is not the water that we use for any of

our adult discus. The adult discus are maintained in reverse osmosis water mixed with city water to create a pH of 6.0 and a microsiemens count of approximately 75.

We have found that eggs removed from breeder tanks with a microsiemens count of 75-80 and placed in hatching

4). The eggs develop a dark eye spot and then begin to hatch. This is a large spawn of over 100 eggs. The eggs hatch in 2-3 days depending on the temperature. The higher the temperature, the faster the eggs hatch. Photos courtesy of Yamada, Mori and Fude from their book *Brand New Discus*.

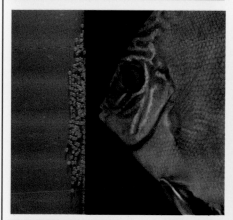

2). The eggs are laid and the parents guard them and fan them constantly with their pectoral fins.

3). The parents are alert to unfertile eggs and usually eat them, leaving the healthy eggs alone.

The discus have selected a PVC pipe upon which to spawn.

The spawning was completed within 20 minutes but the male takes a bit more time to ensure that fertilization took place.

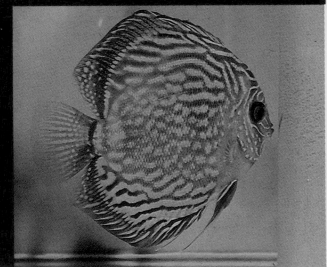

water with a microsiemens reading of 250 suffered no ill effects. Likewise, a pH change from 6.3 to 7.0 caused no problems. We did experience egg losses of seventy-five percent when eggs went from a 7.0 pH to a pH of 6.2 or 6.3.

To the one-gallon hatching containers we add fourteen drops of methylene blue 1%. With this amount of methylene blue in the container it is not necessary

Above: Red turquoise discus with a typical spawn having been laid on a PVC pipe. Photo and fish by Ken Reeves.

Below: A close up of discus eggs. The dark eggs are perfectly normal eggs in various stages of development. The dark spots are the pigmented eyes. The white eggs are infertile and will die. The dead eggs will be attacked by *Saprolegnia* fungus which might spread to the healthy eggs unless you follow Wattley's suggestions by using methylene blue and formalin.

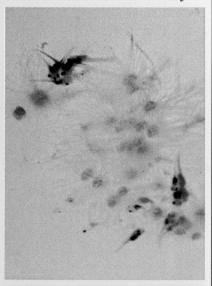

Out of 30 discus eggs only 8 hatched because the fungus *Saprolegnia* attacked the spawn and it was untreated.

to further shield the spawn from light. Methylene blue is a mild bactericide, sufficient to inhibit most bacterial problems in the water. On rare occasions a form of fungus, usually *Saprolegnia*, can cause great harm to the eggs, in which case a fungicidal remedy such as 37% formalin can be used. The formalin dosage depends entirely on the hardness (microsiemens) of the water in the hatching container. The softer the water the lesser amount of formalin will be used. Although we have never

experienced a problem with *Saprolegnia*, if by chance we did encounter it a dosage of two drops of formalin per gallon with a microsiemens count of 200 would be administered.

What about water temperature and aeration in the hatching aquarium? We maintain the temperature at the normal range of 82-84°F, as in the rest of the hatchery, but at two different times of the year the water temperature for the hatching fry will rise to 90°F or more.

The first period is during the hot summer months of July and August when the outside temperature will reach into the 90's. The other period is during the coldest months, generally January and February, when it is necessary to turn on the hatchery gas heater. Since the heater is directly over the hatching area, the water temperature for the eggs and fry will rise to 90°F. Is this higher-than-normal temperature detrimental in any way? Needless to say, it does accelerate the hatching of the

Above:
The feeding pans used by Wattley of white enamel, 11 inches in diameter and 3 inches deep. There is gentle air supplied to each pan.

Below:
A photomicrograph of a newly hatched discus fry.

discus eggs, but we have not found that it causes any subsequent problems. The newly-hatched fry do beautifully in their 90 degree Fahrenheit water, with increased appetites and activity, so perhaps it is somewhat beneficial to maintain that high temperature for a short period. I would not recommend it for an extended period, however.

The eggs are kept in the one-gallon hatching container with a very light flow of air over the top of the container. Strong air flow is not necessary.

Are the eggs kept in the methylene blue water until they hatch? No. During the hatching process we remove the eggs from time to time in order to examine them while still attached to their PVC tube. They are removed from the container for the last time after approximately fifty-two hours and placed directly into clean, clear water in the feeding pan. At this point the eggs have yet to hatch,

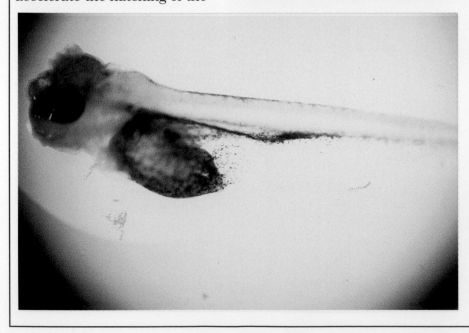

Though Wattley's prefers a hospital white pan, almost any glass bowl will work. Prof. Dr. Axelrod uses his wife's porcelain soup dish much to his wife's objections!

although development will have progressed to the point where it is no longer necessary to keep them in the methylene blue water. Another reason to transfer the eggs to the feeding pan before hatching is that it is easier to remove the spawn while it is still attached to the PVC tube, rather than to have to remove the tiny fry, some of which will have fallen to the bottom of the container.

FEEDING PANS

The feeding pans used in our hatchery are of white enamel, with an inside diameter of eleven inches and a depth of three inches, purchased from a local hospital supply house. If the white pans are not available, glass bowls can be substituted satisfactorily, although we prefer the white pans because the fry can be viewed more easily.

By the sixtieth hour all the eggs should have hatched in the feeding pan, with the fry moving faintly on the PVC tube. The discus fry are now established in their pan and are firmly attached to the PVC sleeve. Although we have not concluded that air in the pan

is necessary at this stage of development, we have not had any more success with air in the pans than without. If air is used, it is gently flowing air from an open airline.

As the discus fry develop on the PVC tube there will be undeveloped eggs, occasionally, as well as malformed fry. Normally these constitute a very small percentage of the entire spawn, but they should be removed from the PVC tube. In our hatchery this is done as frequently as necessary, even daily.

Jack Wattley changing the water in the feeding pan. 40% of the water is changed 2-3 times a day. Photo by Dr. H.R.Axelrod.

At the same time that the developing spawn are being observed it is important to make partial water changes in the pan (although while the eggs are in the methylene blue in the hatching container no water changes are necessary). A slow drip system can be used for the water changes in the pan, or manual water changes can be made using a small plastic cup or a siphon

tube. How many changes should be made each day, and what percentage of the water should be changed? In our hatchery we make two or three changes daily with each one approximately forty percent. There have been occasions, however, when it has not been possible to make any water changes until the end of the day, and neither the eggs nor the fry suffered any ill effects.

THE EGGS HATCH!

An important point to remember is that eggs or fry that fall from the spawning receptacle prematurely are usually indicative of an extremely weak spawn. This is probably due to a genetic problem with the adult fish or can be traced to poor water quality. Nevertheless, soon after the first twenty-four to thirty-six hours, the almost continual wiggling of the fry as they become stronger will cause the majority to begin to release themselves in a normal manner from the PVC spawning tube and fall to the pan bottom. We keep at hand, at all times, a surgical glass syringe with a one-sixteenth inch opening, available from a medical supply house. The syringe is used to remove any remaining fry from the PVC tube by carefully directing a flow of water on them.

At this time, with all the discus fry now at the bottom of the pan, remove the PVC and any debris in the pan, and sit back to wait for the fry to rise up from the bottom. This waiting period will be approximately forty-eight hours, depending on water temperature, during which time the daily partial water

Right: The eggs hatched by the Wattley Method hatch about the same time as those eggs left alone with their parents, but the work of feeding the fry is tremendous when compared to nature's way.

Far Right: In nature's way, the baby discus feed from the slime coating the sides of both parents

Below: Father Discus caring for his recently hatched fry. Photos by Yamada, Mori and Fude from their book *Brand New Discus.*

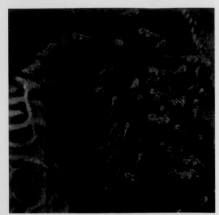

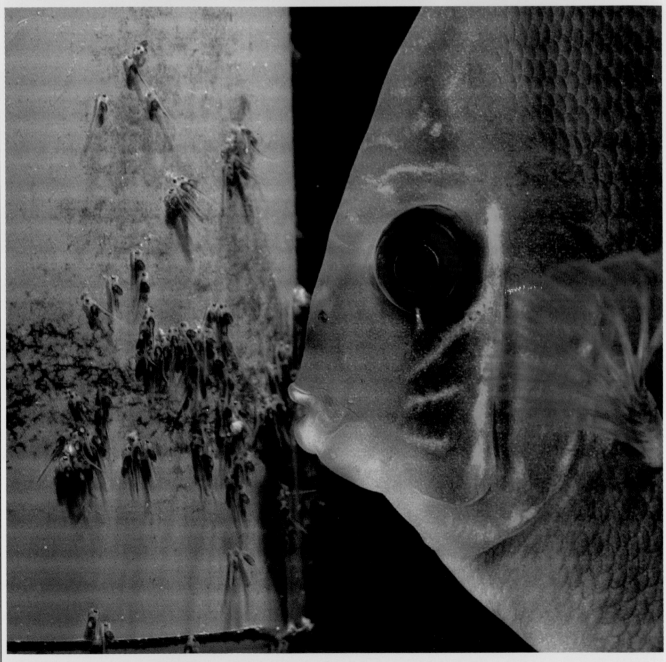

There is no comparative pleasure to watching baby discus feed from their parents' sides. Photos by Petersman.

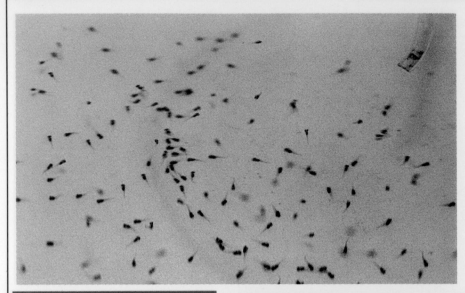

changes should be continued. We use water from our three-hundred gallon holding tank, being careful to ensure that it is the same temperature as the water in the pans.

During the time that they fry are at the bottom of the pan they will nearly always be found clustered in little balls. This is good! When the fry are dispersed throughout the pan bottom, rather than clustered in the ball-like clumps, a weak spawn is usually indicated with many losses to be expected.

Above: When the fry are dispersed over the entire bottom of the pan, it might mean trouble.

Right: Developing discus fry still attached to the spawning site, hardly looks like a discus.

Below: It is a healthier sign when the fry stay clumped together on the bottom of their feeding pan.

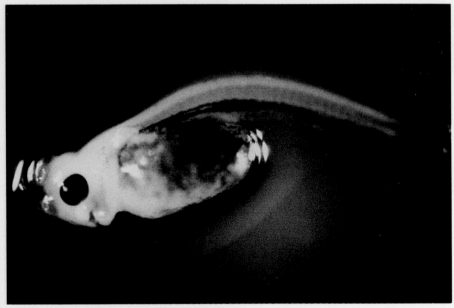

The term *"weak spawn"* indicates a pair of discus spawning in spite of adverse conditions. Such conditions may be an inadequate feeding program for the adult pair over a prolonged period, or perhaps poor water conditions that barely permit a spawning of the pair, with the result being very weak, underdeveloped offspring. A weak spawn can also be the result of the adult pair being too highly inbred. Even crossing a healthy, wild-caught discus with a highly

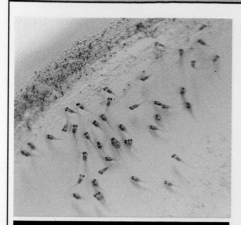

Above: Start feeding the fry when they come up from the bottom of the pan to the surface. Photo by Dr. Herbert R. Axelrod.

inbred weak one will more than likely result in poor future spawns.

FREE SWIMMING

Finally, after much patience and waiting on the part of the breeder, the discus fry will begin to disengage themselves from their clumps and move about the bottom of the pan. *This is definitely not the time to begin a feeding program.* The initial movement around the pan bottom can continue for four hours or longer, with the fry breaking away from their

experimented with many different foods for the discus fry's first several days. Some of this nourishment consisted of nothing more than egg yolk, whereas other foods were formulas consisting of two or more combined ingredients. During this time we initiated a system of coded and numbered control feeding pans in which the fry in each

Below: When the first few fry discover the food and start eating, the other fry will soon join them. Photo by Dr. Herbert R. Axelrod.

Below: The baby discus quickly put on weight and size when they start feeding. Compare these fry to their size one day earlier as shown in the photo on the top of this page. Photo by Dr. Herbert R. Axelrod.

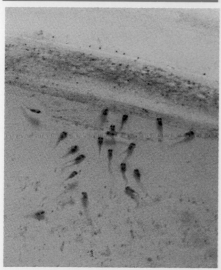

THE JACK WATTLEY FORMULA IS EGG YOLK, *SPIRULINA* AND *ARTEMIA*.

clusters little by little and eventually moving up to water level. If an attempt to feed the fry is made at this time, while most are still at the bottom or near the bottom of the pan, the tiny, almost invisible food particles will cover and smother the fry even before they reach the surface, resulting in the death of many of the young fry.

FEEDING

The initial feeding can be made when the majority of the fry have reached, or are close to reaching, the surface of the pan. Over the years we have

pan received a different food. All data were recorded daily into a log book to determine which formulas resulted in the highest growth rates. At the present time we are certain that our formula is the most complete food for the discus fry's first three to four days of feeding.

The main ingredient in the Jack Wattley Formula is egg yolk, from eggs available at any supermarket. To the egg yolk we add *Spirulina* powder and crushed newly-hatched *Artemia*. We will begin with one raw egg yolk and one hard-boiled egg yolk. (In our

Discus fry never seem to overeat even though they spend a lot of time eating.

this time siphon a sufficient amount of newly-hatched *Artemia*, and after rinsing it in fresh water place it on the paper towel to remove as much water as possible. Add the *Artemia* to the egg yolk/ *Spirulina* mixture, combining all three ingredient thoroughly. Mixing the formula can be done easily in

AN EXCESS OF *SPIRULINA* MAKES THE FORMULA LOSE VISCOSITY CAUSING IT TO POSSIBLY FALL INTO THE BOTTOM OF THE PAN.

hatchery we prepare a large number of yolks at one time, but to simplify our discussion, we will start with one raw yolk and one hard-boiled yolk.) Both yolks are necessary, for neither will adhere to the sides of the pan without sticking, and the raw yolk will do nothing more than to cloud up the water in the pan. However, mixing the two will result in a sticky paste that will adhere nicely to the pan sides throughout the day. At this point you might ask what we do with the hard-boiled egg whites? We do not dispose of them but chop them up into our salads!

After the yolks have been made up into the sticky paste, enough *Spirulina* powder, which is very dark green, is added to change the color of the yellow yolks to a very light yellow green. Because eggs of different sizes—small, medium, jumbo—will be used, we will not recommend here an exact amount of the *Spirulina* powder to add to the yolk paste, which could affect

the balance between yolk and *Spirulina.* An excessive amount of *Spirulina* will reduce the viscosity of the paste, causing it to eventually fall to the bottom of the pan. (The same condition will occur, later, if too much *Artemia* is added to the mixture.) The egg yolk/ *Spirulina* mixture is now ready to form into a flat patty, placed into a plastic bag, and frozen.

As was stated earlier, the time to begin the feeding procedure is after the discus fry have risen from the bottom of the pan. It might be wise to practice administering the formula on a pan with no fry, as it may take several trials runs before the formula is applied correctly. After having made a few trail runs in pans with no fry, you are now ready to begin to raise discus fry using the most successful methods practiced by professional breeders.

Remove the egg yolk from the freezer, thawing it on a clean, white paper towel. At

the palm of the hand, making certain, of course, that the hand is first clean and dry.

The addition of the *Artemia* will alter the color of the egg yolk/*Spirulina* mixture. How much *Artemia* should be added? One part *Artemia* can be added to four parts of the egg yolk/*Spirulina*, approximately. It might be necessary to experiment a bit with the proportions. As with

You cannot tell how the discus will grow until they are 4-5 months old. All baby discus look alike.

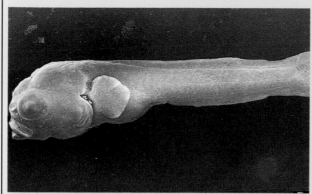

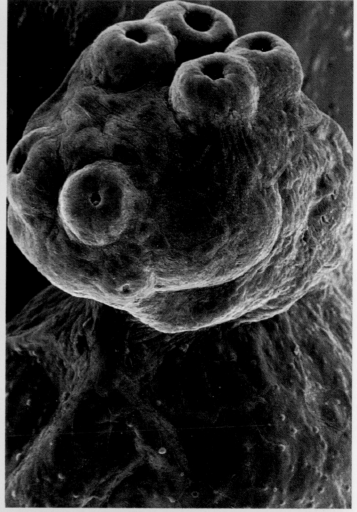

Above: A Six day old discus. The cement glands are relatively small, but the eye, mouth and olfactory organs are already well developed. Photomicrograph by Dr. Harry Grier.
Right: The head of a 3 day old discus, on the day of hatching, showing three magnificent pairs of well developed cement glands by which it attaches itself to the spawning site. Photo by Dr. Harry Grier.
Below: On the day this discus hatched, the pectoral fin is a mere bump seen at the dorsal edge of the yolk sac. A gill slit is visible, but the mouth has not formed as yet. The large knobs on the head include the developing eye and the developed cement glands. Photo by Dr. Harry Grier.

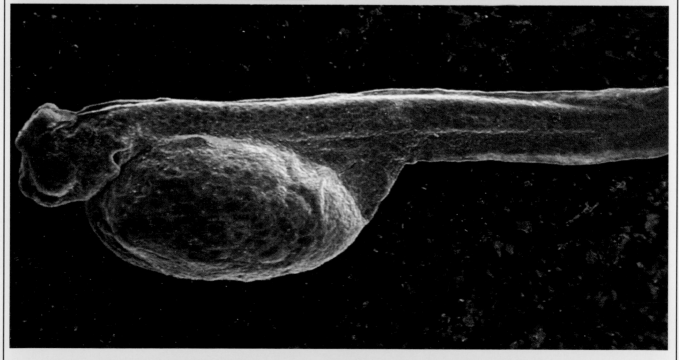

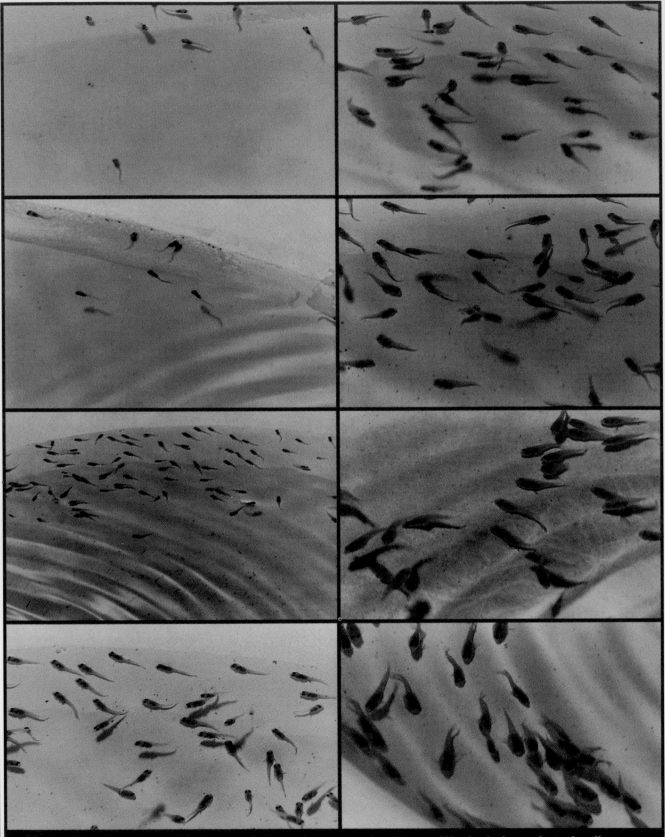

The feeding evolution of the free-swimming from from feeding on Wattley's formula to feeding on newly hatched brine shrimp, *Artemia*. Photo by Dr. Herbert R. Axelrod.

the *Spirulina*, if too much *Artemia* is added to the yolk mixture, the food will not adhere properly to the sides of the feeding pan.

Partial success can be experienced without the addition of the *Artemia* to the egg yolk, but we have found that the formula is more complete with the *Artemia*. Minimal success can also be had by initially feeding the fry only the *Artemia*, but the *Artemia* alone is not an adequate diet for the growing fry.

The egg yolk/*Spirulina*/ *Artemia* formula will result in accelerated growth for the discus fry, with a higher-than-normal growth rate than for discus fry that are raised with the parents. We have frequently observed discus fry feeding from their parents next to tanks with fry hatched artificially. The fry in both tanks were the same age. We have seen a greater growth rate for the pan-raised fry after three to four days.

When the fry are ready to feed for the first time you will find, unfortunately, that in most cases they will rise from the bottom of the pan in the morning, having completely absorbed their egg sacks. Three full days is usually sufficient time for the fry to feed on our formula, although if they begin to feed later in the day it is a good idea to add three more full days of formula feeding before proceeding to the next food. In trials we have advanced to the next food after just two days on the formula, but have found that the third day of formula feeding is very important for the fry.

The feeding pan should now be siphoned down approximately half-way and the upper half completely dried with a clean, dry paper towel. After mixing the formula in the palm of the hand, take a small amount and with a finger of the other hand, make a thin bead about three-eighths of an inch in

THREE DAYS IS ENOUGH FOR THE FRY TO BE FED ON WATTLEY'S BABY FORMULA. THEY NEED NEWLY HATCHED BRINE SHRIMP AFTER THAT.

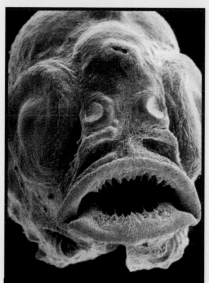

The head of a six day old discus shows well developed teeth. The cement glands are rapidly disappearing at this age, but the eyes and olfactory organs are well developed. Photo by Dr. Harry Grier.

width, applying the food thoroughly yet carefully all around the inside of the pan. It generally takes four or five strokes to use all the formula in the hand when forming the ring around the top of the pan.

The formula is applied as thinly as possible, and while three-eighths of an inch in width is certainly adequate, narrower is better, although it can be very difficult to apply a more narrow bead than that.

Under no circumstances raise the water level to the top of the pan immediately after the formula has been applied to the sides and the fry are still on the bottom half of the pan. A fifteen-minute drying period is necessary for the formula to adhere properly to the pan sides for the twelve-to-fourteen hour feeding program. Furthermore, if the formula has not been applied correctly it will fall into the water, making it necessary to lower the water level, wipe off all the food from the sides of the pan, siphon the remainder of the food that fell to the bottom of the pan, and start all over again!

After the drying period has been completed the water level can be carefully raised to the top of the pan, covering the formula. If, for any reason, there is extreme humidity in the room it may be necessary to allow the food to dry for a bit longer. A method of hastening the drying process can be accomplished by the use of an electric fan over the feeding pan. Some experimentation may be necessary, however, because if the food is allowed to dry too much it will quickly become too hard for the fry to eat even when submerged for a period of time.

WATER CHANGING

After the water level has been raised to the top of the pan the discus fry will be ready to begin their initial feeding. Pan water temperature should be 82-86°F or higher. With a formula consisting primarily of egg in that warm water, the bacteria count will climb rapidly unless you add a mild bactericide.

In our hatchery we add, to the pan filled to the top with water, approximately twenty milligrams of Furan-2, a bactericide consisting of sixty milligrams of nitrofurazone, twenty-five milligrams of furazolidone, and two milligrams of methylene blue. With the addition of the correct amount of Furan-2, it is a powder in capsule form, the water can be added directly to the pan. We have found that it is much easier to make a stock solution first, adding the desired amount directly to the pan, saving the remainder for subsequent water changes.

In all cases, we begin to feed the fry at approximately 7:30 a.m., if they have risen from the bottom of the pan by that time and have begun to swim about. If a feeding is made at that time it will not be necessary to change the water again until approximately 1:00 p.m.

In the center of the pan is a plastic air line with just enough air to gently break the water surface. Twenty-five to thirty air bubbles per minute will accomplish this. We have never found air stones to be suitable because many of the fry tend to hover around the stone rather than to move to the pan sides to feed.

MANY SPAWNS ARE EATEN BY THE PARENTS. THAT'S WHY WATTLEY'S METHOD IS SO VALUABLE.

No one has been successful in taking the fry from the parents at the free swimming stage and raising them by Wattley's method.

At 1:00 in the afternoon it is time for a water change. What if it is impossible to make the 1:00 change? After many trials we have found that delaying the water change by an hour or even longer did not harm the spawn. Make the water change by 10:00 a.m. or so, and by doing so your next water change would be made around 4:00 p.m.

The length of time between water changes can be determined by the depth of the pan and the amount of water in the pan. The more water there is in the pan, the more time can be allowed between water changes.

FURTHER FEEDINGS

If the outlined procedures are followed correctly, with no interruptions, the last feeding will be made at approximately 7:00 p.m. In making all water changes it is best to siphon out as much water as possible, leaving the fry just enough water to cover them. A fresh application of Furan-2 must be made at the time of each feeding. The last water change can be delayed to 1:00 a.m. or so if you want to watch the late night movie on television.

Around 11:00 p.m. we remove all food from the pan for the night. Again, siphoning out as much of the water as possible and with a clean paper towel, remove all food from the sides of the pan as well as any food particles that may have fallen to the pan bottom. It is important to remove all residual formula before filling the pan with fresh water. It is not necessary to add the Furan-2 during the night. Our hatchery room that houses the breeding stock and advanced juveniles contains no night-time lighting system, although there is a dim light near the pans in the room with the fry.

The second day operation is

to be conducted exactly as on the first feeding day. By this time you should be able to see a bit of growth in the fry, and by the beginning of the third day most of the fry should have doubled in size. There will no doubt be some losses of fry, especially in the first three or four attempts at raising them, but as the procedure is refined fewer losses should be experienced. With experience, the only fry you may lose will be the few which are deformed. These deformed discus fry are easy to detect. Most will have either a curvature of the spinal column or an elongated stomach area. By the second or third day these few defective fry will still be alive. If and when these fry are detected in the pan they should be humanely

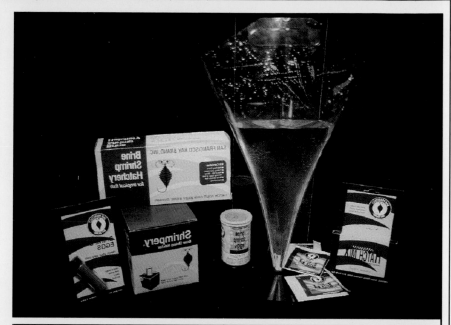

All of the equipment and supplies needed to hatch out baby brine shrimp from eggs are easily obtainable at pet shops. Photo courtesy of San Francisco Bay Brand.

The well written and easily understandable book on diseases of discus, *DISCUS HEALTH* by Dieter Untergasser is TFH number TS-169 and is available at most pet shops.

destroyed.

If the parent fish have successfully raised their own young, there should be no difficulty in artificially raising fry from a subsequent spawning. But if the fry show no discernible growth by the second day of feeding, or certainly by the third day, then there is the possibility that perhaps the parent fish have internal parasites. With a microscope, which you should own if you are serious about discus keeping, and referring to T.F.H. book TS-169 Discus Health by Dieter Untergasser, you should be able to determine if your fish are free of harmful parasites, e.g., *Hexamita*. It is important to remember that all fish have normal intestinal flora. These microorganisms that coexist

with the fish, so if you do encounter microbes under the microscope it does not necessarily indicate a problem.

CHANGING DIETS

You have now completed the third day of feeding the formula with no procedural changes and are now ready to move to the next stage. At this time the discus fry should be able to take newly-hatched *Artemia*. Shortly after introducing the *Artemia* you will be able to detect it in the fry. While ingesting the egg formula the fry will appear to be a light gray in color, but within a short time after introducing the *Artemia* you will see their color change to a pale orange. This will be very noticeable if you are using a white enamel pan. If you do

EIGHTY PERCENT OF DISCUS FRY ACCEPT *ARTEMIA* AFTER THE FOURTH DAY.

A male adult fairy shrimp can only be fed to a discus 2 inches long. Male fairy shrimp have large heads and live in fresh water so they can only be offered to discus 2 inches or larger.

ONCE THE FRY EAT *ARTEMIA*, THEIR BELLIES WILL TURN ORANGE AND THEIR GROWTH WILL SPURT.

accept *Artemia* on the first day of feeding, but a better quality discus can be produced by continuing the formula for the complete three days, as stated earlier.

The correct procedure for introducing the *Artemia* is completely different than the egg formula feedings. The *Artemia* will not adhere to the pan as the egg formula does, and therefore when applied to the top of the pan will simply fall to the bottom or to the sloping sides near the pan bottom. When that occurs the fry will be at the top of the pan with the *Artemia* food at, or near, the pan bottom. Therefore, it is necessary to lower the water level in the

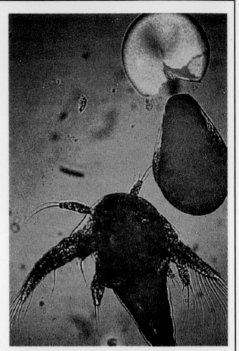

Newly hatched *Artemia* (brine shrimp) showing the egg, the nauplii and a shrimp one hour old. Photo by Artemia Research Center.

not see this color change take place after twenty minutes or so, it will be necessary to continue the egg formula for another day. What frequently occurs is that the faster-developing fry will take the *Artemia* on the fourth day, while other fry will not. This will be very apparent to the eye as some fry will be orange in color while others in the same pan will remain gray.

In our hatchery we find that if approximately eighty percent of the fry have accepted the *Artemia* on the fourth day we then proceed with *Artemia* feeding, but with the strong possibility of losing most of the remaining twenty percent. One method to save the fry that did not accept the *Artemia* is to transfer them to another pan for the fourth day egg feeding. We have had many spawns that are able to

Brine shrimp, *Artemia*, at double life-size, are ideal foods for all tropical fishes. Photo courtesy of San Francisco Bay Brand the world's largest packer of brine shrimp.

pan to approximately one inch to one-and-a-quarter inches for the first several days of *Artemia* feedings. At that depth the *Artemia* will be on the lower sloping pan sides and the fry will begin to feed immediately.

Common sense must be used when adding the *Artemia* to the pan. An overabundance of baby *Artemia* will most certainly smother and kill most of the fry. Conversely, there must be sufficient *Artemia* for the fry to feed on as they move about the pan. Live *Artemia* also utilize the oxygen in the pan, so it is necessary to continue to use the air line.

At this point the Furan-2 is no longer necessary because the *Artemia* will not pollute the water. How long should the *Artemia* be left in the water before a water change is necessary? We leave it in the pans until mid-afternoon, at that time siphoning out all that remains, and in the process siphoning out most of the water as well.

Although the life span of the *Artemia* in fresh water is several hours, it is not necessary to remove any that have died until the routine mid-afternoon water change. In that short period of time there is no danger of any pollution, and the discus fry will continue to consume the dead *Artemia*. Fresh, newly-hatched *Artemia* that have died in the pan are much more nutritious than frozen baby *Artemia*, so there is absolutely no need to worry about the few hours that the fry consume any dead *Artemia*.

After the mid-afternoon water change the next one will be done at night, when all remaining *Artemia*, fecal matter, and any other debris will be removed. The pan should be filled to the top for the night, with no more food given until the following morning. The next morning the water level is lowered again, after which time the *Artemia* are added again.

By the third day of the *Artemia* feedings the water level can be gradually raised, until after another two or three days when the water can be raised to the top of the pan. By this time the fry will begin to disperse more freely

throughout the pan and will begin to actively seek out the *Artemia*. In another three or four days the growing fry will be able to be moved to larger quarters.

We move the fry at this time into glass aquariums of two gallons, as we can control the feedings more easily by using small tanks. A five-gallon tank would no doubt be acceptable,

BABY DISCUS REQUIRE 3-4 DAYS OF INTENSIVE FEEDING WITH *ARTEMIA* NAUPLII.

The popularity of discus has led manufacturers and processors of frozen foods for aquarium fishes to make specialized discus food available to hobbyists and breeders. Photo courtesy of San Francisco Bay Brand.

although it is not advisable to move the fry from the pan to anything larger than five gallons. It is important to continue to use the air line in the center of the tank.

The length of time that the

fry are kept in the two-gallon tank depends largely on the number of fry in the spawn; the larger the spawn, the less time the fry will be kept in the tank. If the spawn totals one hundred fry or more they are kept there no longer than a week. As in the pans, several daily water changes are made, removing any debris at that time.

From the two-gallon tanks the fry are normally moved to twenty-gallon tanks, which are the same size that our discus pairs are housed in. There have been occasions when all the twenty-gallon tanks have had other discus in them, and we have moved the fry directly into our seventy-five gallon "grow out" tanks with no subsequent problems. Regardless of whether the fry go directly to the twenty-gallon tank or to the seventy-five gallon tank, they adjust very quickly and within minutes will accept food.

When the fry are moved to larger tanks, filters are used for the first time. We use sponge filters, which are very easy to maintain. Because most of the sponge filters available are of the vertical air-lift variety, a word of caution is in order. Up to this point the young discus have not had to contend with heavy water turbulence, but a too-strong water turbulence resulting from improper use of a sponge filter can cause heavy fry losses, especially during the first seven to ten days in the new aquarium.

After the move to a larger tank the fry are introduced to our Jack Wattley Discus Fry Food. With all discus, regardless of size, the introduction of any new food must not be made in an abrupt manner. We introduce fifteen to twenty percent of our fry food at the same feeding as that of the newly-hatched *Artemia*. Discus fry adjust fairly quickly to a new food, by the afternoon feeding or no later than the following morning the fry will have accepted the formula. When it is evident that the fry are taking the new food the quantity of *Artemia* given previously can be reduced. We have always found that our young discus develop better on the frozen formulated diet, rather than on a diet of *Artemia*, exclusively.

It is my hope that this information, which includes the most current techniques for successful raising of discus fry, will be of use to the beginning discus fancier eager to venture into the exhilarating experience of raising discus from eggs. Likewise, the more experienced discus breeder who is seeking to refine already-established hatchery procedures for greater success will surely benefit from the point-by-point recommendations made here, the result of our efforts to create a better discus.

YOUNG DISCUS DEVELOP BETTER ON FROZEN FORMULATED DIET THAN ON *ARTEMIA* ALONE.

The Jack Wattley Discus Formula fish food is made by Ocean Nutrition according to Wattley's formula. Wattley himself doesn't sell the food. Every complete pet shop offers this frozen food product.

LIST OF DISCUS BOOKS YOU SHOULD READ

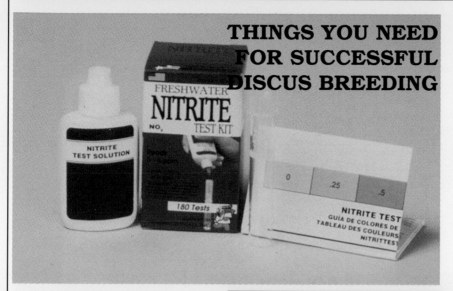

THINGS YOU NEED FOR SUCCESSFUL DISCUS BREEDING

This chapter did not exist in the original text and is supplied to help non-German aquarists since many of the German products are not available outside of Germany.

To better identify certain products, we have listed the name of the manufacturer. The products suggested here are available at your local pet shop. Often pet shops are more knowledgeable about local conditions and might recommend a substitute product. In all cases *follow the advice of your local pet shop expert.*

▲ Testing for nitrite concentration in freshwater aquariums is simple with this kit. Photo courtesy of Aquarium Pharmaceuticals.

WATER

Nothing is more important in a discus tank than the water it contains. Not only must the water be clean and clear, it must also have the correct acidity (pH), and be free of poisons, like the nitrites chlorine and

▼ You can change the water in your aquarium every week, more or less, but you must maintain control by checking the pH. Photo courtesy of Aquarium Pharmaceuticals.

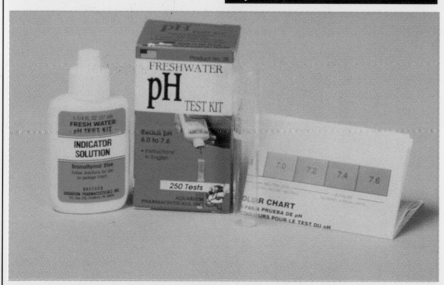

ammonia. There are test kits available to test for these toxic substances. There are also solutions to neutralize the toxins, but unquestionably the best treatment for any water problem is to change up to 50% of the water every few days and replace it with aged water of the proper pH and temperature.

Changing water *in the old days* meant buckets being carried between the tank and the bathroom! No longer!! There is a device called an *Automatic Water Changer* which makes water changing

▲ Aquarium Pharmaceuticals has a master test kit which enables you to check all the parameters necessary to maintain a healthy aquarium.

a *no-hands* operation. This one gadget has done more for the aquarium hobby than any other single product.

When the fish require treatments for ich or fungus and a dye is used, the water becomes discolored. If your tank is located in your living room and heavy tobacco smoke or cooking odors permeate the air you pump into your tank for aeration, you will need to remove these

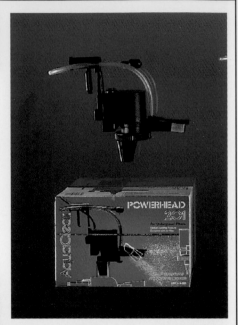

The Hagen AquaClear Powerhead ▶ increases the water movement in multiples. It is a real help in keeping Discus healthy.

FILTRATION

There are many kinds of filters available for the discus tank. Obviously, the kind of filtration depends upon the size of the tank. The usual rule with discus tanks is:*It can't be too large, it can only be too small.* That's what made the 1,000 gallon double bull nose aquarium so popular

▼ American Acrylic, San Diego, CA can make a tank of any size and any dimension. Can you imagine a 5,000 gallon tank filled with huge Discus?

▲ The best gadget ever invented for the lazy aquarist is an automatic water changer. Photo by Aquarium Products.

gases or colors from the water. The best way to do this is with Biochem Zorb which absorbs the colors and gases which are so detrimental to the health of your discus.

▼ Special nylon pouches filled with high quality filter medium is offered by Aquarium Pharmaceuticals.

with real discus aficionados. The tank comes complete with stainless steel stand and cabinetry. Obviously this needs special filters. In the usual tanks, especially those with undergravel filters, powerheads increase the flow of water many times, depending on the strength of the powerhead.

The Hagen BioLife wet/dry filtration ▶ system is ideal for discus tanks.

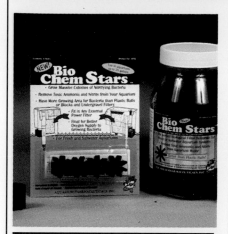

▲ Discus require pure water and Bio Chem Stars helps keep water pure. Photo courtesy of Aquarium Pharmaceuticals.

A new development in filtering is the Bio-Chem Stars. These are biological filter material that provides a home for growing massive colonies of nitrifying bacteria. These bacteria convert waste to nitrites and the nitrites to nitrates which are plant fertilizers. These Stars are added to the external filters and convert it to a sort of wet/dry filter system. It seems to be wonderful for discus tanks.

HEATING THE WATER

You can filter the water and

▼ The Hagen Thermal Heater line features well tested thermostatically controlled heaters in many sizes.

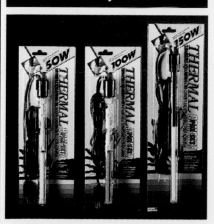

make sure that it is perfectly pure for discus, but if it isn't of the correct temperature, your discus will die! Discus requires temperatures between 80° and 85°F. The 85°F. mark is for breeding; the lower temperature is for normal activities. The only practical way to keep a discus tank heated is with a thermostatically controlled heater. By far, the best such heaters are the submersible type which are also thermostatically controlled. The Thermal line of heaters come in sizes of 50 watts to 300 watts, in 50 watt steps. It is difficult to say which wattage you should use because that will depend upon the size of your aquarium and the ambient room temperature. If your room doesn't get colder than 60°F. and you have a 50 gallon tanks, then a 300 watt heater will suffice. If the room temperature drops to 50°F. at night, you may need two 300 watt heaters. If you are keeping a small, 10 gallon aquarium with some young discus, you might only need a 50 watt heater, providing the room is kept at 75°F.

Having the heater is often not enough. The heater only heats the water immediately surrounding it. You really have to heat the whole tank. This is best done with an air pump. The air pump is connected to an air stone or other air outlet by means of a plastic tubing. The outlet is placed near the heater so it spreads the heated water more or less uniformly throughout the aquarium. The air pump also aerates the aquarium at the same time. No discus tank can operate

▲ The Whisper Pump made by Tetra/Second Nature is available in capacities that are suitable for any discus tank

satisfactorily without an air pump.

DISCUS FOODS

Discus in the wild are limited to what they can forage. They usually don't move very far from their protective area among dense vegetation. This means they can't be accustomed to a great diversity of diet. Each discus expert has his own food secrets. Jack Wattley, America's leading discus breeder, has developed a food for discus which he sells through Ocean Nutrition. This is a frozen food and works very well. Hikari, on the other hand, offers frozen bloodworms. These are wonderful for discus once they become accustomed to eat it. Offer them these bloodworms when they are hungry, after fasting them for a few days. Once they eat them, they'll love them and they are the closest food to the worms they eat in nature.

Boyd Enterprises makes a

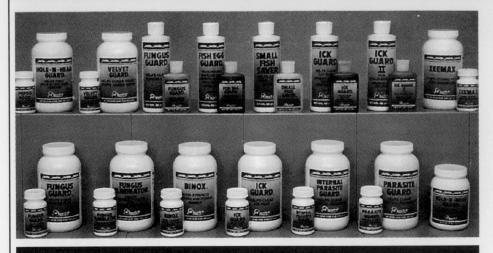

▲ Jungle Laboratories offers a complete range of remedies and preventatives.

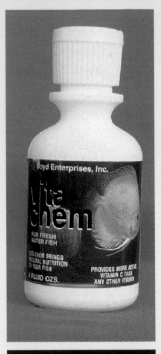

▲ Boyd Enterprises makes a complete line of marine salts and special discus water treatments.

Vita-Chem which is really a vitamin for discus. They have a discus on the label and seem to have a positive effect on the health of discus. Pet shops use this vitamin for their own discus.

HEALTH

You can have perfect water, perfect food and think you're doing everything right when all of a sudden the fish become ill. Of course it's always at night after your local pet shop has closed. What to do? Your pet supplier can help you build a first aid kit for discus. It should contain many different remedies, preventatives and tonics. Talk to your dealer and follow his advice.

We are NOT suggesting that you treat your fish every time you THINK there is a problem. What we are trying to communicate is that you should be PREPARED should a problem occur. This is especially true of parasites; most people don't quarantine their fishes before they add them to their well

established tank. They know they should, but they don't. Sooner or later they will pay the price when a disease or parasite strikes!

Remember, also: *An ounce of prevention is better than a pound of cure!*

▲ Hikari makes a complete line of frozen foods ideal for discus. Their bloodworms is a favorite.